# KITCHEN, STITCHIN'

*Chris Malone*

©2005 Chris Malone
Published by

**kp books**
*An Imprint of F+W Publications*

**700 East State Street • Iola, WI 54990-0001**
**715-445-2214 • 888-457-2873**

Our toll-free number to place an order or obtain
a free catalog is (800) 258-0929.

Library of Congress Catalog Number: 2005924816

ISBN: 0-87349-944-1

Designed by Emily Adler
Edited by Sarah Herman

Printed in China

# Dedication

I dedicate this book with all my heart to my mother, who understood how much I liked "to make stuff." She always gave me encouragement and praise and displayed *all* my completed projects *forever*, even when I begged her to take them down.

# Acknowledgments

Many thanks to the kind and talented people at KP Books, especially Sarah Herman, my extra-patient and always-cheerful editor; Julie Stephani, the acquisitions editor who encouraged me to take on this challenge; and Bob Best and Kris Kandler, the skillful photographers who took all the photos for this book.

I also want to thank Amy and Scott Wisner, who welcomed us into their beautiful home for many of the photographs and Hansen's Brand Source in Waupaca, Wis., who also endured our cameras, lights, cords and boxes so we could use their wonderful furniture for some of the settings.

And I thank my husband Jim for stepping over piles of fabric, putting up with my late hours and eating at the kitchen counter because the dining table was covered with projects in progress. Now it's time to decorate my own table again!

# Introduction

When I think of family gatherings, I picture my gang around the dining table; it's a center of energy and camaraderie for us. And I believe the dining table is a symbol of hospitality and togetherness for most families, large and small. It's where we celebrate holidays, special occasions, victories and accomplishments and where we entertain our friends. Decorating our tables and our kitchens then, is one very special way we have to create a warm and inviting atmosphere for the people we care about.

This book is a collection of nine themed sets for kitchen and table décor. Each chapter theme features four to seven coordinating projects. There is a chapter for each season and also for special times including a tea party, coffee klatch, family dinner, celebration event and card party. Every chapter has a table covering of some kind along with other related pieces such as a napkin and napkin holder, appliquéd towel, cookie jar, lined and decorated basket, wine bag and many more. Much of it is easily interchangeable, such as using the flower motif from A Bloomin' Table on the winter cookie jar lid or on the recipe album from the Family Fare chapter.

In this book, I share many favorite techniques that I hope you will enjoy learning and will find inspiration to use again and again. Included are silk ribbon embroidery, rag-hooking, quilting, appliqué—even a little fabric decoupage and stamping—and all are clearly explained and illustrated with photos and diagrams.

Since choosing the fabrics for a project is such an important step and can be intimidating for many, I have a section at the beginning of each chapter explaining the fabric choices I made and how they affect the style of the collection. Some chapters visually show how using the same pattern, but changing the fabric, can dramatically alter the result.

Please take time to become familiar with the supply list and the basic techniques; then enjoy making your own kitchen and table décor!

# Table of Contents

# Basic Supplies

*If you have been sewing long, you probably already have most of the tools listed here and are well on your way to a pretty good stash of fabrics to choose from. If you are just starting out, this chapter should give you some basic direction to acquiring what you need and what will make each task easier. The right tools and the appropriate fabrics and embellishments ensure success and make the process a lot more fun!*

## Materials

*Fabrics, batting and threads are the bones of these projects and their level of quality makes a big difference in the final result. A better grade cotton fabric is smooth, even and closely woven with strong threads; a good batt will lay flat and wash well; and higher grade threads are much easier to sew with. The embellishments are the frivolous parts that add fun and flavor to any project.*

### Fabrics

For me, choosing the fabrics for a project is both the most stressful part of the process and the most fun. I probably pull out 10 fabrics for every one I end up using and I have noticed many times how substituting one fabric for another can make a striking difference in the final result. The three attributes of fabrics for our purposes are *color, pattern and texture*. Each property plays a role in determining the mood of the collection.

Bright, lively colors set a playful stage, perhaps for a family birthday party, while soft pastels seem most appropriate for an afternoon tea party. Combining a garden of florals in a project will have a far different effect than using only geometric prints. Fabrics with a polished finish or metallic highlights will be more formal than homespuns.

In each chapter, I have a short section called "Fabric Selection," in which I explain how I chose the fabrics for that theme. Two chapters show the dramatic difference made by interpreting the same theme with a very different collection of fabrics. The chapter titled "Autumn Leaves" has a formal table runner with napkins and napkin holders using beautiful fall-colored fabrics, some with a shiny finish and metallic copper highlights. Using the same leaf motif and the same colors, but substituting homespuns and osnaburg with more visual texture, the look is cozy and informal. In the chapter titled "Let's Celebrate," the table runner and accessories are black-and-white geometrics with just a touch of red for a sub-

dued and sophisticated look. The place mat in that chapter is also made from geometric print fabrics, but the colors are vivid and lively and the result is a totally different mood.

> Please note that in some projects, traditional cuts of fabric yielded too many leftovers. Therefore, some projects require "fat quarters" of fabric to minimize waste. A fat quarter is an 18" x 22" cut of fabric. Some projects also require scraps. For all of these projects, a scrap will mean at least 12" square. Please refer to the cutting instructions to see the specific sizes you will need for each fabric.

### Battings

There are so many types of batting available—cotton, wool, silk, polyester, blends, high-loft, low-loft, needle punched, fusible—and every experienced quilter has her favorites. Since the designs in this book are for the kitchen and dining room, and most will be laundered again and again, I used a needled polyester batting for most of the projects. Sometimes I selected a high-loft polyester for a puffier look. If you are new to quilting, I suggest that you make a point of trying different kinds of batting to see which works best for you.

### Threads

Any project can only be as good as the quality of the materials in it. This applies to thread, too. Good quality thread is smooth, strong and feeds through the machine evenly. Save the "bargain" spools for basting.

### Embellishments

Buttons, beads, ribbons, flowers, floss, trims, wire and anything that can be tied on, sewn on or glued on that adds interest and dimension is fair game!

# Tools

*A rule of thumb that I have learned to follow is to always buy the best quality tool I can afford. It will pay for itself by working better and lasting longer than the cheaper alternative. That said, nothing lasts forever and it is also important to know when to change needles or blades, sharpen scissors and oil moving parts. Buy the best, take good care of it and your reward will be far less stress and superior results!*

## Sewing Machine

A basic sewing machine with a good, reliable straight and reverse stitch is all that is needed for any of the sewing projects in this book. If you wish to appliqué by machine instead of by the hand techniques used in my models, you will need a machine with a zigzag stitch (or the blanket stitch on some of the newer models). A ¼" foot is very helpful in piecing and a walking foot or free motion quilting foot is important if you plan to machine quilt. A zipper foot is needed for sewing on some trims.

Follow the instructions in your machine's manual for cleaning, oiling and other maintenance tips to keep your machine in good working order.

## Scissors

A good, sharp pair of scissors for fabric and a second, cheaper pair for paper, cardboard and template plastic is essential. A smaller pair of embroidery scissors is handy for snipping threads.

## Rotary Cutter and Mat

A rotary cutter and mat are not necessary for these projects, but they certainly help make the cutting process quick, easy and accurate. Always use a cutting mat when using a rotary cutter to protect your tabletop and the blade of your cutter. Buy the largest size mat you have room for; a 24" x 36" mat is a good size for most sewing projects. A small mat can be very handy for cutting and trimming small pieces. Choose a rotary cutter with a handle that is comfortable in your hand. The 45mm blade is favored by most quilters. For efficiency and safety, change the blade whenever it becomes dull or nicked.

## See-Through Ruler

There are many shapes and sizes of see-through plastic rulers on the market. A good all-around size is the 6" x 24" with ¼" markings and a 45-degree angle line. A smaller ruler, such as a 6" x 12" or a 6" square, is useful for smaller pieces.

## Thimble

This is such a personal choice that there is no right or wrong answer. There are thimbles made from metal, leather and plastic in many forms and sizes. It is a good idea to try several, but I can almost guarantee that you will not immediately fall in love with any of them. It takes time to get used to using a thimble, but it really will protect your sewing finger (the one that pushes the needle in) and you will grow to appreciate your thimble even if you never love it! I prefer a leather thimble with a small metal disc at the fingertip.

## Marking Tools and Templates

A pencil for marking light fabrics, a fade-out pen for tracing embroidery patterns and a white pencil for marking dark fabrics should be part of your basic supplies. Template plastic (available in quilting shops) or lightweight cardboard, such as recycled file folders or gift boxes, can be used for pattern templates.

## Needles and Pins

For machine sewing, check the needle package and use the size recommended for the fabric you are sewing. Be sure to change needles as soon as they show signs of dullness. An embroidery needle, size 8-10, is necessary for hand stitching with embroidery floss. For hand quilting, a needle called a "between" is recommended. Use the size most comfortable for you; 7-10 are the most common sizes. For hand appliqué, a "sharp," in sizes 10-12, is the best choice.

## Quilting and Embroidery Hoop

A quilting hoop, which has deeper bands than an embroidery hoop, is very useful to hold the three layers of fabric and batting taut and smooth while quilting. For quilting just the borders around a small project, however, I usually do not use a hoop. Embroidery hoops in several sizes are inexpensive and good to have on hand for projects that include embroidered embellishments.

## Fusible Web

This is an iron-on adhesive that is transferred to the wrong side of a piece of fabric, making it possible to fuse that fabric appliqué to a background. All brands differ somewhat, so follow the manufacturer's instructions for ironing.

## Freezer Paper

This is one of my favorite tools for cutting felt shapes and preparing fabric appliqués. It's available in grocery stores and now in many savvy quilt shops as well.

## Iron, Ironing Board, Towel and Pressing Cloth

When you are sewing and quilting, a good steam iron is your friend and ally. The finished project will look so much better if the seams have been crisply pressed at every step. A towel is useful when pressing embroidery, because if the embroidered section is placed face down on the towel, the stitches will not flatten with the pressure. I use a pressing cloth with fusible web and when one or more of the fabrics is heat sensitive.

# Basic Techniques

*Many of the techniques used in these projects are repeated and those techniques are detailed in this chapter. Please take the time to read and understand each process before starting the projects in the book and refer back to them as needed. Some of the procedures described are not the only way to accomplish a task, but are my favorite ways. If you prefer, feel free to substitute your own methods. Mastering the basic techniques will make the projects go quickly and smoothly.*

## Rotary Cutting

A rotary cutter, mat and see-through ruler make it possible to cut strips and patches accurately and quickly. Start with a smooth piece of yardage (ironed if necessary, because wrinkles will distort the cuts).

1. Fold the fabric in half lengthwise, with the folded edge closest to you and the excess fabric to the right. Align a smaller ruler, such as a 6" x 12" or 6" square, with the fold of the fabric near the edge to be trimmed and place your 12" x 24" ruler right up against the left side of the smaller ruler. The long ruler should just cover the raw edge of the fabric.

2. Remove the smaller ruler without disturbing the long ruler. Make your first rotary cut along the right edge of the ruler, holding it firmly in place with your left hand. Use firm even pressure as you cut. Always cut away from yourself.

3. To cut strips, align the appropriate vertical line of the long ruler with the cut edge of the fabric and the folded edge. For example, if you need a 4"-wide strip, line up the 4" vertical line with the cut edge of the fabric and any horizontal line on the ruler with the fold. When it aligns exactly, cut along the ruler edge.

4. To make squares or rectangles, as for many of the patchwork projects in this book, first make a strip the correct width. Then, use the smaller ruler to cut the strip into squares or rectangles.
If you are left-handed, work from the other end of the fabric and reverse the directions.

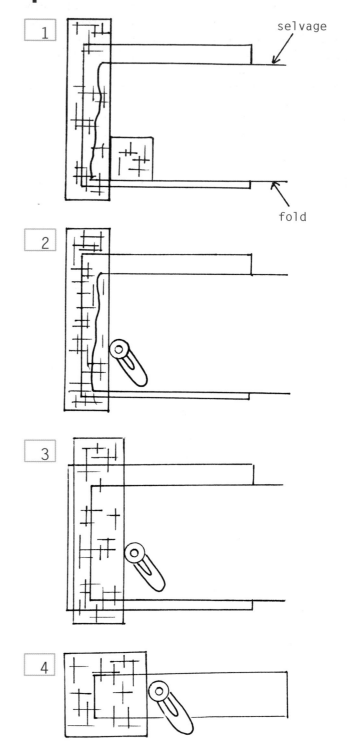

selvage

fold

## TIPS FOR ROTARY CUTTING

1. Hold the ruler steady. Placing your little finger off the ruler onto the work surface will help prevent the ruler from slipping while you are cutting.

2. For safety, always roll the cutter away from yourself and keep your fingers away from the blade. Get in the habit of closing the safety guard on the blade after every cut.

3. Stand comfortably, with your body centered over the cutting line to make your cuts.

4. For a long cut, stop the cutter and move your left hand up on the ruler. Resume cutting.

5. If the rotary cutting system is new to you, practice on some scrap fabric until you get a feel for the technique.

# Piecing

All cutting instructions in this book include a seam allowance in the measurements. This will always be ¼" unless otherwise stated. It is as important to maintain an accurate seam allowance as it is to cut accurately, so everything fits together properly. If your machine does not have a ¼" foot, sometimes referred to as a quilter's foot, you can mark the throat plate on your machine with masking tape placed exactly ¼" from the center of the needle. Unless otherwise directed, all seams are sewn with the right sides together. Measurements given for borders and backing assume accurate cutting and seam allowances. It is a good idea to measure your patchwork before cutting the border strips or backing pieces; if there is a difference, you will need to adjust your cutting measurements accordingly.

## TIP

Fabric is easier to handle when it is starched. Spray starch and press the fabric pieces before piecing, and the fabrics will be less prone to shifting. I usually spray starch fabrics that have a lot of give, such as homespuns, before piecing.

1. To start a beginning seam without snarling the threads or having the fabric pulled down into the needle hole, hold on to the two tail threads as you start to sew. Or you can use a scrap of fabric to begin the seam. Sew through the scrap and then right into the seam allowance of the pieces being joined.

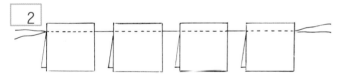

2. For the quickest piecing and to save thread, use a technique called "chain piecing" to sew a number of sets at once. To chain piece, sew one set of pieces together and stop at the edge of the fabric. Without lifting the presser foot, slip the next set of pieces under the toe of the presser foot and continue the seam without clipping the threads. When finished with all the sets, remove them from the machine and clip the threads between each set.

3. Many quilting guides will say it is not necessary to lock your stitches by reversing at the beginning of the seam if another seam will later cross that seam and hold it. I prefer, however, to reverse just one or two stitches at the end because the seam can begin to pull open when it is being handled and can be a nuisance.

## BASIC SEWING SUPPLIES

| These are the basic supplies that are needed for every chapter: | | |
|---|---|---|
| ◇ Sewing machine | ◇ Ruler | ◇ Assortment of sewing needles and pins |
| ◇ Iron and ironing board | ◇ Scissors for fabric and paper | ◇ Marking tools and templates |
| | | ◇ Thimble |

# Pressing

Always carefully press after each seam. This will flatten the seam and make it easier to join the next pieces with accuracy.

1. Iron the unit in the closed position (as sewn) to set the stitches.

2. Carefully open the unit and press with the iron in an up-and-down motion (sliding the iron across the fabric can stretch and distort the seam).

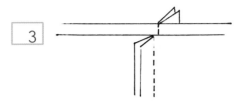

3. Traditionally, the seams are pressed to one side, usually toward the dark side. When you are going to be joining two rows of pieced units, press the seams on one row to the right and the seams on the other row to the left. When you pin the two rows before sewing, simply slide the seams together until they match perfectly. The slight thickness of the seams will hold the matched seams close.

# Backing, Batting and Basting

Adding the backing and batting to the pieced top is sometimes referred to as "sandwiching," an apt term for combining these three layers of a quilted project. The instructions for the individual projects give the measurements for cutting the backing and batting.

1. Press the pieced top and the backing fabric.

2. Spread out the backing, wrong-side up, on your work surface and smooth out all the wrinkles. Carefully place the batting over the backing and then add the pieced top, right-side up, on the batting.

3. Insert pins or safety pins about every 10" or so. Pins may be adequate to hold the layers of a small project in place, but I prefer to baste everything with thread. If it is basted, you can move, and even fold it, without shifting the layers. Basting stitches are simply long running stitches with a single strand of thread. First baste about ⅛" from the outside edges, starting with a knot or backstitch and ending with a backstitch. Baste about every 6", avoiding the places that will be quilted. After the quilting is completed, these basting threads are easily pulled to remove.

# Binding

All of the quilted projects in this book are finished at the edges with either an applied binding or, for smaller projects, with a technique called self-binding. Usually, I quilt a project before using the applied binding method, but with self binding, quilting is the last step.

## Self-Binding

In this technique, the backing, batting and top are layered in a different manner.

1. Place the batting on the work surface first, smoothing it out with your hands. Place the backing right-side up on top of the batting and cover it with the pieced top, right-side down.

2. Sew all around with ¼" seam (unless otherwise directed) and leave an opening along one edge for turning.

3. Clip the corners and trim the seam allowance of the batting close to the seam. Turn the item right-side out.

4. Fold in the seam allowance on the opening and hand sew the opening closed. Press the top well.

## Applied Binding

Double-fold applied binding consists of two layers of fabric and is the most durable edge finish you can use, which is important for projects that will be used and laundered.

1. Cut the binding strips as indicated in the instructions for each project. The binding strips can be cut on the lengthwise or crosswise grain unless the binding will be applied to curves. Then it is preferable to cut the strips from the bias of the fabric (diagonal to the grain). All the binding for the projects here can be cut on the straight grain unless bias binding is specified.

2. Usually it is necessary to join two or more strips to obtain the total length necessary. To eliminate bulk, join the strips with a diagonal seam. This is easy to do by pinning the ends at right angles to each other. Sew a diagonal seam and trim the excess, leaving ¼" seam.

3. Fold under 1" at one end of the binding strip; press. Fold the entire strip in half lengthwise, wrong sides together, and press.

4. Beginning along one side, place the folded binding (with the hemmed end) against the right side of the quilt top, matching the raw edges. Start sewing about 2" from the end of the binding, sewing through all the layers with ¼" seam. Stop sewing ¼" from the first corner of the quilt. Backstitch, then clip the threads and remove the piece from under the sewing machine presser foot.

5. Fold the binding upward, creating a 45-degree diagonal fold and finger press.

6. Bring the binding back down, matching the raw edges and aligning the top fold with the top of the quilt. Begin sewing at the very edge of the top, sewing through all the layers.

7. Sew all around the quilt, turning and mitering each corner in the same manner.

8. When you reach the beginning point, slip the binding strip's raw edge inside the folded end (you will need to trim the binding so it will overlap the starting point about 1"). Fold the binding over the raw end and finish stitching it down.

9. To finish, bring the folded edge of the binding over the raw edges to the back. Hand stitch the binding to the backing fabric. Use a small stitch and be sure to cover the machine stitching with the binding. To miter the corners on the back, hand stitch up to a corner and fold the binding strip into a miter and secure with a few small stitches.

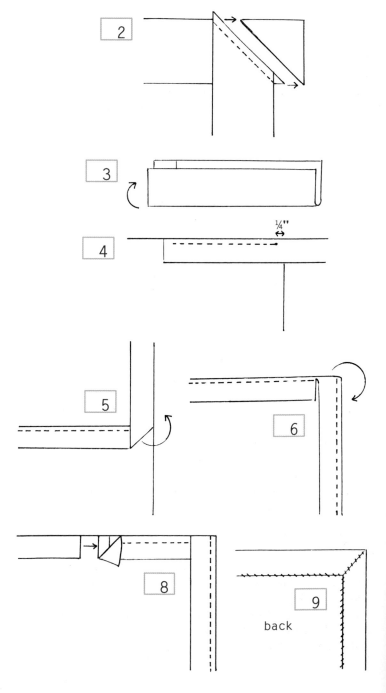

# Quilting

Most of the quilted projects in this book are hand quilted, usually along the seams or "in the ditch." Hand quilting is simply a small running stitch that holds the three layers of backing, batting and top together. The size of the stitch is not as important as the evenness, which comes with practice.

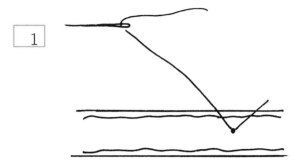

1. Thread your quilting needle with an 18" length of quilting thread. Tie a small knot at the end of the thread. To start stitching, bury the knot in the batting so it doesn't show on the outside. Insert the needle into the quilt top going into the batting, but not through to the backing. Bring the needle back up exactly where you wish to begin quilting. Tug gently on the thread to "pop" the knot through the top and leave it buried inside the batting.

## TIP

That finger on the underside gets pretty sore after a session of hand quilting! There are several remedies for this besides cultivating calluses (which does help). A small piece of masking tape or the reusable sticky plastic ovals sold in quilting shops work the best for me. Some quilters use a spoon to push the needle back up.

2. Wear a thimble on the finger that will push the needle through (usually the middle finger of your dominant hand) and place your other hand underneath the quilt to guide the needle back up. Push the tip of the needle down through the three layers and as soon as your finger on the underside feels the needle coming through, tip the needle up again toward the top. Use this "rocking" motion to stack two to three stitches on your needle, then pull it through. Pull the thread taut, but not so tight that it puckers the fabric.

3. When you have nearly run out of thread or are ending a section of quilting, wind the thread around the needle two times to make a small knot. Press the tip of the needle on the quilt, pull the knot close to the fabric, and insert the needle into the batting (but not through to the backing). Come up again ½" away, pulling the knot into the layers in the same way as the starting knot. Pull the thread gently, clip it close to the fabric, and the end should disappear inside.

# Fleece Padding

For some smaller shapes that are sewn all around with padding inside, I use a simple method to accurately sew and turn these pieces. When it is completed, the piece is evenly padded and the shape is smooth along all the outside edges.

1. Cut two pieces of fabric and one of fleece at least ½" larger all around than the pattern.

2. Trace the pattern on the wrong side of one of the fabric pieces.

3. Put the two fabric pieces right sides together, with the drawn pattern on top; pin together with the fleece on the bottom.

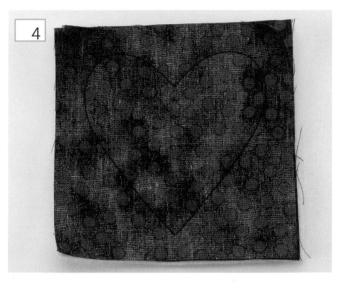

4. Sew all around on the pattern lines.

5. Cut out the shape about ³⁄₁₆" from the seam. Trim any corners and clip the curves.

6. Using a small sharp pair of scissors, cut a slash through one layer only of the fabric large enough for turning. Apply a fray-preventative to the cut edges if this slash will not be completely covered later. Let the solution dry before turning the shape right-side out.

7. Press well and slip stitch the opening closed.

# Appliqué

*The word "appliqué" means literally "to apply," as in applying one layer of fabric to another. It is a wonderful way to add unique decoration to a simple towel or a complicated patchwork top. I prefer to hand appliqué, to hand sew my fabric shapes on with small, invisible stitches or with decorative blanket stitches. If you prefer to machine appliqué, any of the appliqué preparation methods I explain here will also work for machine stitching, such as a satin stitch or one of the decorative stitches available on some machines. I have found that the time spent preparing my appliqués is worth the effort, making the hand stitching easy and enjoyable. I am going to show you my favorite methods of preparing and sewing appliqués using either iron-on fusible adhesives or freezer paper.*

## Fusible Appliqué

This is certainly the easiest method of appliqué, as it does not require turning under edges and can even be completed without any added sewing if you choose.

### Fusing: Method 1

1. Trace the appliqué pattern onto the paper side of the fusible web (the pattern must be reversed at this stage so it will face the correct way when fused to the fabric). If drawing more than one shape on the paper, leave a margin of at least ½" between the shapes.

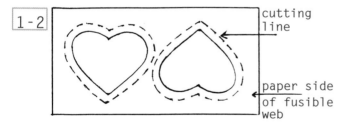

2. Cut out each shape loosely about ¼" from the traced lines. Do not cut out on the pattern lines.

3. Follow the manufacturer's instructions for the proper iron setting and the times for fusing, as each type varies. Place the shape on the wrong side of the appliqué fabric with the fusible web against the fabric and the paper side up. Fuse the shape to the fabric by pressing.

4. Cut the appliqué shape out on the traced lines, cutting through the paper and fabric. Remove the paper backing and you will see the shiny fusing film that has transferred to the fabric.

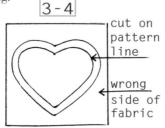

5. After cutting out all the pieces for the appliqué design, arrange them on the background fabric. Refer to the photo and the pattern of the appropriate project for guidance. The dashed lines on the patterns indicate appliqués that overlap slightly. To "fine tune" the arrangement and get each piece exactly where you want it, use a pin or needle to pull the appliqué into position. When everything is arranged to your liking, fuse it all in place with the iron.

### Fusing: Method 2

Fusible web can make larger appliqué shapes rather stiff for some projects. To prevent this, use this alternative method for cutting out the shape.

1. Trace the appliqué pattern onto the paper side of the fusible web (the pattern must be reversed at this stage so it will face the correct way when fused to the fabric). If drawing more than one shape on the paper, leave a margin of at least ½" between the shapes.

2. Cut out the center of the paper shape, leaving just ¼" border inside the pattern line. This leaves enough adhesive to attach the edge of the appliqué, but the center remains free of adhesive and soft to the touch.

3. Cut out the appliqué, remove the paper backing and fuse the appliqué in place.

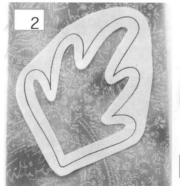
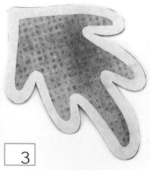

### Finishing

If you used the heavyweight, or "ultra," fusible web and do not wish to add hand stitching, the appliqué is complete! If you wish to machine finish the edges, always use the lightweight sewable version. This version is also suitable for hand finishing, although my personal preference is to use the medium- or heavyweight even when I hand blanket stitch the edges because I like the extra adhesive. Use two to three strands of embroidery floss or one strand of size 5 or 8 pearl cotton to outline the edges of the appliqué with a simple blanket stitch, described on page 14.

# Freezer Paper Appliqués

I don't know who first thought to move her role of freezer paper from the kitchen into the sewing room, but it was a marvelous idea! The shiny, waxy side of freezer paper will adhere to the fabric when it is ironed on and is still easy to remove when it is no longer needed. I use it when I want an appliqué with the edges turned under. There are two basic ways to prepare appliqués with freezer paper—with the shiny side up or the shiny side down.

## Fusing: Shiny Side Up

**1.** Trace the appliqué pattern on the dull side of the freezer paper.

**2.** Cut out the pattern directly on the pattern lines.

**3.** Cut a piece of fabric about ¼" larger than the pattern on all sides.

**4.** Center the paper on the wrong side of the fabric with the shiny side up. If there are inner points, as on a heart or star, clip into the seam allowance almost to the pattern line. Use a hot, dry iron along the edge of the appliqué to push the seam allowance up and over the freezer paper. The paper will stick to the seam allowance and hold it in place. If there is a point on the appliqué, as on a leaf or a corner, press the point straight up and over the edge, and then press each side to make a clean sharp point.

**5.** When the appliqué shape is well-pressed and has cooled down, gently pull back the seam allowance and remove the paper. Re-press the seam allowance.

*Note:* I sometimes brush a bit of spray starch onto the seam allowance, pressing it dry before removing the paper. Spray the starch into a container and use a small brush or cotton-tip swab to dampen the fabric.

## Fusing: Shiny Side Down

**1.** Trace the appliqué pattern on the dull side of the freezer paper.

**2.** Cut out the pattern directly on the pattern lines.

**3.** Iron the freezer paper shiny-side down on the wrong side of the fabric. Cut the fabric out about ¼" from the edge of the paper.

**4.** Clip any inside points and press the seam allowance up and over the freezer paper with the edge of a hot, dry iron. If there is a point on the appliqué, like a leaf or a corner, press the point straight up and over the edge, and then press each side to make a clean, sharp point.

*Note:* I like to use a needle and thread and baste the seam allowances before pressing. With the basting step, you can carry a baggie of appliqués to work on when you have a few minutes. Ironing is then a quick step. If you wish to add spray starch, add it at this point.

**5.** When the appliqué shape is well pressed and has cooled down, gently pull back the seam allowance and remove the paper. Re-press the seam allowance.

## Finishing

After the freezer paper is removed, the appliqué is ready to be sewn to the fabric background by hand or machine. Use a blanket stitch or an "invisible" appliqué stitch to attach the shape.

**1.** Thread a small thin needle with a single strand of sewing thread and make a small knot at the end.

**2.** Pin the appliqué to the background and make tiny stitches from the edge of the appliqué straight into the background and up again at the edge of the appliqué about 1⁄16 "-1⁄8" away. Pull each stitch taut without puckering the fabric.

# Stitch Details

*I use five embroidery stitches repeatedly in the projects in this book. They are simple to learn and master. The blanket stitch is used for some appliqué finishes and on the edges of felt cutouts. The running stitch, backstitch, French knot and stem or outline stitch are basic embroidery stitches that I use to embellish some of the projects.*

## Blanket Stitch

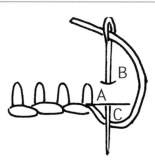

Use this stitch on the edge of an appliqué or to finish the edge of a cloth. The needle comes out at A on the edge. Insert the needle into the appliqué or cloth at B and back out at C, again on the edge.

## Running Stitch

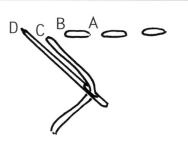

Bring needle up at A; go down at B creating a straight stitch. Come up at C, go down at D, leaving a space between B and C.

## Backstitch

Bring the needle up at A, one stitch length away from the starting point of the line you are stitching. Insert the needle down at B and bring it up at C. Repeat, inserting the needle at the end of the stitch just completed (in the same hole).

## French Knot

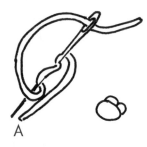

Bring the thread up at A. Wrap the thread around the needle two times and hold the thread taut. Insert the needle back into the fabric very close to the same point. Pull the needle down through the fabric, leaving the knot on top.

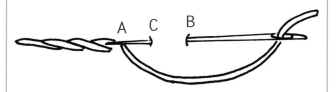

## Stem or Outline Stitch

Bring the needle up at A. Insert the needle down at B, about ⅛" away from A. Bring the needle up at C, down at D, and up again at B.

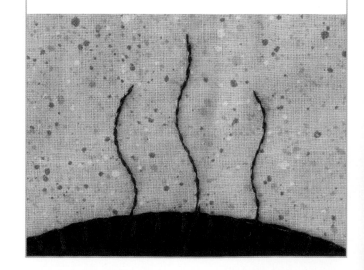

# Napkin Finishes

*Since the focus of this book is on kitchen and table items, you will see many napkins, but I used only four different finishing methods. The fringed and hemmed edge versions are one layer of fabric, while the reversible and the reversible-with-border are made with two different squares of fabric. I particularly like the versatility of the reversible napkins since they can be so much fun to fold and manipulate. My napkins are usually 16"-18" square, but you may prefer a larger napkin, or a smaller one such as the size of a cocktail napkin. Just change the cut size to suit your preference and adjust yardage needs accordingly.*

## Fringed Edge

1. Cut the napkin to size.

2. Using matching thread, sew all around ⅜" from the edge.

3. Use a pin to pick out the rows of threads and pull off rows until you reach the stitching line. *Note:* It is important to cut on the grain of the fabric to make a neat fringe.

## Hemmed Edge

1. Cut the napkin to size.

2. Press ¼" hem all around.

3. Fold the hem again so it is doubled and press well.

4. Use a few pins to hold the hem in place and stitch all around.

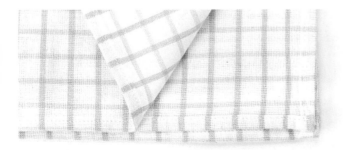

## Reversible Napkin

1. Cut two napkins to size using two different, but coordinating, fabrics.

2. Pin the two squares together, right sides together, and sew all around with ½" seam allowance. Leave a 4" opening along one side.

3. Trim the corners and turn right-side out. Press well.

4. Fold in the seam allowance on the opening and hand sew the opening closed with a small whipstitch from edge to edge.

5. Topstitch ¼" from the edge. *Note:* You can use a different top and bobbin thread if you wish to have either contrasting or matching thread on both sides.

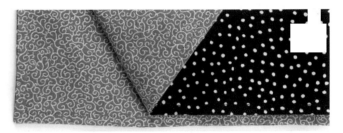

## Reversible Napkin with Border

1. Cut two different, but coordinating, fabric squares, one 4" larger than the other.

2. Place the largest square wrong-side up on the work surface. Center the smaller square on the larger, right-side up. Pin or baste the two squares together.

3. Press ¼" hem all around the larger square. To miter each corner, fold and press a corner of the large square up and over the corner of the smaller square. Trim this fold to about 1".

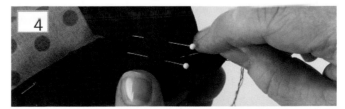

4. Fold each side over the edge of the small square and pin the mitered edges down. Use matching thread to hand sew the folded edges together.

5. Finish the napkin by topstitching close to the fold of the border with matching thread.

# A Bloomin' Table

Have a spring fling and whip up a set of quilted place mats, reversible napkins and flower napkin holders to welcome the season. The centerpiece of the table arrangement is a hooked table mat and matching coasters made with strips of fabric, burlap and a traditional rag-rug hook. An appliquéd tea towel hanging smartly from a wooden spoon is cute and handy, too.

## FABRIC SELECTION

The black-and-white fabrics offset the bright red, green and yellow accents. The combination is fresh and invigorating—much like the season itself. If you were to substitute fabric prints in shades of rose, soft leaf green, pale yellow and cream, the collection would take on a softer feeling.

# Hooked Table Mat and Coasters
Finished size: 10½" x 21" mat, 5" - 5½" coasters

## MATERIALS

(for one table mat and four coasters)

Fabric:
- ◊ 1⅛ yd. red print
- ◊ ½ yd. yellow print
- ◊ ⅝ yd. dark green print
- ◊ 1⅛ yd. medium green print
- ◊ 1½ yd. burlap
- ◊ 1½ yd. tan felt for backing

Stretcher bars:
- ◊ 16" stretcher bars: 2
- ◊ 20" stretcher bars: 2
- ◊ 9" stretcher bars: 4 (or substitute an 8" embroidery hoop for a small frame)

Rag-rug hook

Staple gun and ¼" staples

Staple remover or table knife

Medium-point black permanent marker

Permanent fabric adhesive

Rotary cutter

Mat

Lined ruler

Patterns:
- ◊ Flower with Leaf, page 22
- ◊ Flower, page 19
- ◊ Leaf, page 22

## CUTTING INSTRUCTIONS

*Note:* Use a rotary cutter, mat and lined ruler to cut strips from the following fabric:

From the red print, cut:
- ◊ 1" strips

From the yellow print, cut:
- ◊ 1" strips

From the dark green print, cut:
- ◊ 1" strips

From the medium green print, cut:
- ◊ 1" strips

From the burlap, cut:
- ◊ One 28" x 36" rectangle

*This hooked table mat and coaster set takes a little time to complete, but the result is so unique and tactile that it is worth the extra effort. I find that working on these hooked projects is similar to processes like knitting or quilting, in that it is repetitive and soothing as you find your own rhythm.*

Become familiar with the hooking techniques on page 20 before beginning this project.

1. Enlarge the flower with leaf pattern 200 percent using a copy machine.

2. Trace the flower and leaf pattern onto the 28" x 36" piece of burlap with the black marker.

3. Assemble the 16" and 20" stretcher bars into a 16" x 20" rectangular frame.

4. Lay the burlap flat on the table, pattern side down, and place the frame on top so the flower and one leaf show completely within the frame. Pull the edges of the burlap over the frame and staple it in place. Start with the center of one side and then move to the center of the opposing side. Staple the center of the other opposing sides; then start adding a few staples in each direction. Staple about every inch, keeping the burlap as taut as possible.

5. Hook the fabric strips as follows, working from the outer edge to the center:
   ◇ Outline the leaf, including the vein line, with dark green
   ◇ Fill in with medium green
   ◇ Outline the flower with red and continue with rows of red until you reach the center section
   ◇ Outline and fill in the center with yellow

6. Remove the staples with a staple remover or table knife and move the frame over so the remaining leaf pattern is within the frame. Staple the edges again, but use just a few staples on the already hooked section, placing them down on the burlap between the loops.

7. Hook the remaining leaf exactly like the first leaf (see Step 5).

8. Remove the staples and take the burlap off the frame.

9. If the mat appears warped or bumpy, wet a towel and wring it out as much as possible. Lay the mat, loop side up, on a flat surface and cover it with the towel. Flatten the mat with your hands. Remove the towel and let the mat dry thoroughly, using weights if necessary to stay flat (I place a large cookie sheet on the hooked project with a few books on top).

10. Remove the excess burlap by cutting about 1½" from the outer hooked edge.

11. To finish the edges, turn the mat over so the back of the mat is facing up. Fold and glue the edge over the back of the mat. Clip almost to the mat edge on curves and inner corners; cut excess burlap out by cutting V-shaped wedges where necessary so the border/hem will lay flat.

12. Use the pattern or the completed mat to cut a backing piece from the tan felt. Glue the felt in place on the back of the mat.

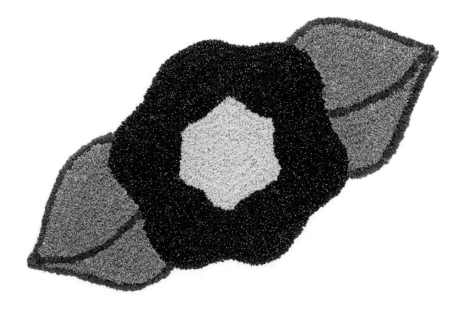

# COASTER INSTRUCTIONS

1. Assemble the 9" stretcher bars into a square frame (or substitute an 8" embroidery hoop).

2. Cut a 15" square of burlap for each coaster and trace a flower or leaf in the center.

3. Attach the burlap to the prepared stretcher frame in the same manner as for the table mat, or place it securely in the embroidery hoop.

4. Follow the same instructions for hooking and finishing the coasters as for the table mat (see page 18).

## TIP

To care for these decorative hooked projects, remove any stain as soon as possible. Dab the stain with a damp cloth until clean. Do not launder or immerse these pieces in water.

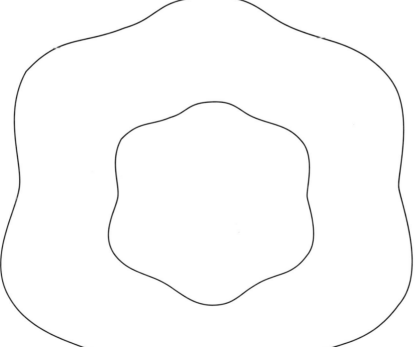

Flower
for Hooked Coaster

*Hooking, or rag work, consists of a technique of making loops with fabric strips using a special tool called a rag-rug hook. This hook has a short, rounded handle with a crochet-type hook on the end. A crochet hook will pull the fabric strips through the burlap, but would be too uncomfortable to use for a project this size. A hook with a latch is also unsuitable. Rag-rug hooks are available wherever rug making supplies are sold. Check the Resources on page 128 for a mail-order source for hooks and all other supplies.*

*Ordinary burlap is satisfactory for these projects, however, a better quality burlap is firmer and more durable and also available through rug making sources.*

*The fabric loops made by the hooking technique are held securely in place by the displacement of the warp and weft threads of the burlap which squeeze the fabric. To work, sit comfortably at a table with part of the prepared frame resting on the edge of the table, right-side up, and with one hand (the non-dominant hand) under the frame. The other hand holds the hook above the burlap. The hand beneath the burlap guides the fabric to the hook.*

**1.** Draw the pattern onto the burlap with a medium point marker pen. Include the inner markings, too.

**2.** Lay the burlap flat on the table, pattern-side down, and place the frame on top so the pattern is completely within the frame. Pull the edges of the burlap over the frame and staple it in place. Start with the center of one side and then move to the center of the opposing side. Staple the center of the other opposing sides; then start adding a few staples in each direction. Staple about every inch, keeping the burlap as taut as possible.

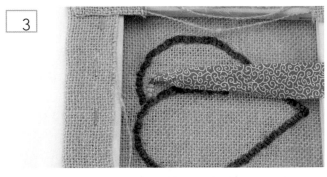

**3.** Hold the end of a fabric strip against the back of the burlap where the pattern starts. Poke the hook into a hole (a gap between the warp and the weft) and pick up the fabric strip with the hook, a few inches from the end of the strip. Pull the end of the strip up through the hole to the top of the burlap; pull enough fabric through to make a tail of about 1", as shown in the photo above.

4. Poke the hook back into a different hole that is next to, or very close to, the strip end. This time when the hook grabs the fabric, pull up a loop about 1" high. Keep the fabric on the hook.

5. Using your hand underneath the burlap, carefully pull the fabric strip back down until the loop remaining is about ¼" high, as shown in the photo above. Remove the hook. Repeat the process by poking the hook near the last loop and pulling up another loop. When hooking a row of loops, skip only one or two threads between the loops. When hooking a row beside an existing row, make the loops close enough to touch without distorting the loops.

6. When coming to the end of a strip, pull the remainder of the strip through to the top.

7. To start another fabric strip in the same row, pull the beginning tail through the same hole as the ending hole of the previous strip. Trim the ends to match the loop height.

8. After removing the hooked piece from the frame and trimming off the excess burlap, glue the burlap edges over the back of the piece, clipping as necessary.

9. Cut a piece of felt to fit the piece and glue it in place.

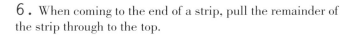

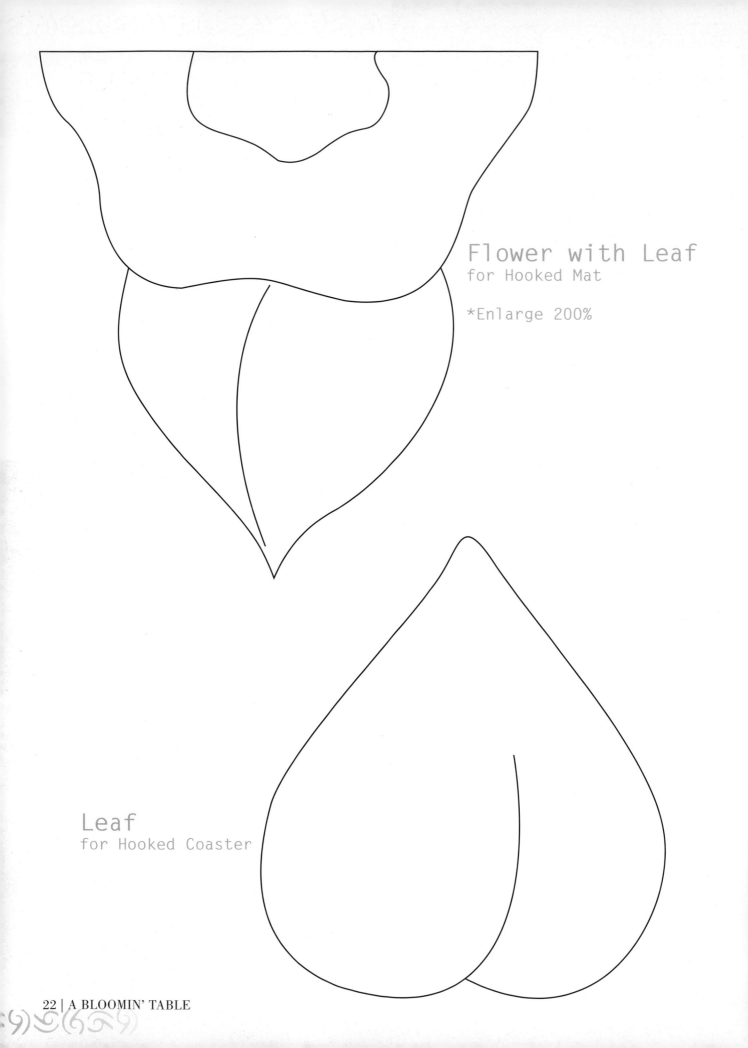

Flower with Leaf
for Hooked Mat

*Enlarge 200%

Leaf
for Hooked Coaster

# Place Mat
Finished size: 16½" x 12½"

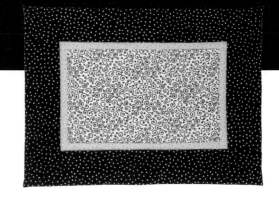

## MATERIALS

(for one place mat)

Fabric:
- ◇ ¼ yd. white with black print for center
- ◇ ⅛ yd. yellow print for inner border
- ◇ ⅜ yd. black with white dots for outer border and backing

17" x 13" batting

Matching sewing threads

Quilting needle

Quilting thread for hand quilting:
- ◇ Yellow
- ◇ White

## CUTTING INSTRUCTIONS

From the white with black print, cut:
- ◇ One 11" x 7" center

From the yellow print, cut:
- ◇ Two 1" x 7" inner border strips
- ◇ Two 1" x 12" inner border strips

From the black with white dots, cut:
- ◇ One 17" x 13" backing
- ◇ Two 3" x 8" outer border strips
- ◇ Two 3" x 17" outer border strips

## INSTRUCTIONS

1. Sew the 1" x 7" yellow inner border strips to each side of the white with black print center panel; press the seams outward.

2. Sew the 1" x 12" yellow inner border strips to the top and bottom of the center panel; press the seams outward.

3. Sew the 3" x 8" black dotted outer border strips to each side of the bordered panel.

4. Sew the 3" x 17" black dotted outer border strips to the top and bottom of the bordered panel.

5. Add the batting and finish the construction of the place mat with the Self Binding technique on page 10.

6. Finish by quilting "in the ditch" (quilting right beside the seam line) between the center panel and the yellow borders using white quilting thread and between the yellow and the black using yellow or white quilting thread.

*This place mat is a simple but perfect complement to the perky flower napkin ring and napkin on page 24. I chose to make it puffy by using high-loft batting. Quilting between the borders gives it dimension.*

# Napkin and Napkin Holder

Finished size: 16" square napkin, 3½" napkin holder

## MATERIALS

(for one napkin and one napkin holder)

Fabric:
- ◇ Fat quarter black with white dots
- ◇ Fat quarter green print
- ◇ Scrap of red print
- ◇ Scrap of yellow print
- ◇ Scrap of fleece

Shank button, 1½" diameter

5½" elastic, ¾" wide

Matching sewing threads

Safety pin

Permanent fabric adhesive

Patterns:
- ◇ Flower, page 26

## CUTTING INSTRUCTIONS

From the black with white dots, cut:
- ◇ One 17" square
- ◇ One 2¼" x 9" strip

From the green print, cut:
- ◇ One 17" square

From the red print, cut:
- ◇ One 4½" x 9" rectangle

From the yellow print, cut:
- ◇ One 2¾" diameter circle

From the fleece, cut:
- ◇ One 4½" square
- ◇ One 1½" diameter circle

*Fold this reversible napkin so a bit of coordinating fabric shows. The hint of color pops against the dimensional flower napkin holder.*

# NAPKIN HOLDER INSTRUCTIONS

**1.** Fold the red print rectangle in half, right sides together, and draw the flower pattern on the wrong side of the fabric.

**2.** Refer to Fleece Padding on page 11 to sew the flower together using the red print fabric and the fleece square. Top-stitch ¼" from the edge with matching thread.

**3.** To make the flower center, glue the fleece circle to the top of the button.

**4.** Finger press a small (⅛") hem along the edges of the yellow circle and hand sew a gathering stitch with a double length of sewing thread all around the hem. Do not knot the thread.

**5.** Place the button in the center of the yellow circle, on the wrong side, and pull the thread so the fabric covers the button and gathers around the shank. Knot the thread, but do not clip it.

**6.** Using the same thread, sew the button to the center of the fabric on the right side (the side without the slash).

**7.** Fold the black dot strip in half lengthwise, right sides together, and sew the long edges together with ¼" seam. Turn right-side out and press the seam so it runs down the center of the strip. Press the seam so it runs down the center of the strip.

**8.** Attach the safety pin to one end of the elastic and push this end through the fabric band, without letting the other end slip inside the fabric.

**9.** Pin the elastic ends and sew the short ends of the fabric and the elastic together with the seamed lines facing. Press the seam open.

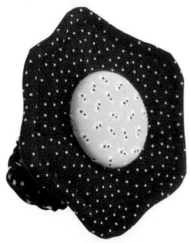

**10.** Glue the wrong side of the flower to the covered elastic band, covering the short seam.

**11.** Fold the napkin diagonally so both fabric sides show and insert it into the elastic band of the napkin holder.

1. Pin the two 17" squares right sides together.

2. Sew all around with ½" seam allowance, leaving a 4" opening on one side.

3. Trim the corners and turn right-side out. Press.

4. Fold in the seam allowance on the opening and hand sew the opening closed with a small whipstitch from edge to edge.

5. Topstitch ¼" from the edge with matching or contrasting thread.

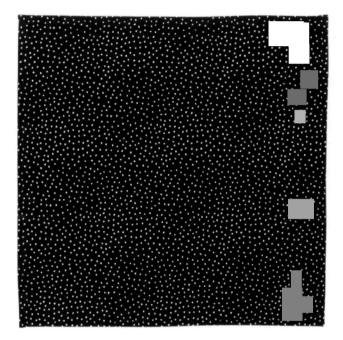

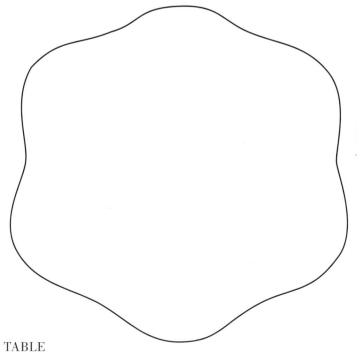

Flower
for Napkin Holder

# Tea Towel and Spoon Holder
Finished size: 20" x 28" towel

## MATERIALS

Fabric:
- Scrap of red print for the flower appliqué
- Scrap of green print for the leaf appliqué

20" x 28" black-and-white checked tea towel

18"-long wooden spoon

Yellow button, 1⅛" diameter

2 yd. black-and-white checked wire-edged ribbon, 1½" wide

Matching sewing threads

White acrylic paint

Paintbrush

Permanent fabric adhesive

Freezer paper

Patterns:
- Leaf, page 29
- Flower, page 29

*This easy towel set is a perfect and useful accessory for the kitchen. The black-and-white checked towel has flower and leaf appliqués and hangs from a painted wooden spoon that is suspended from a black-and-white checked ribbon.*

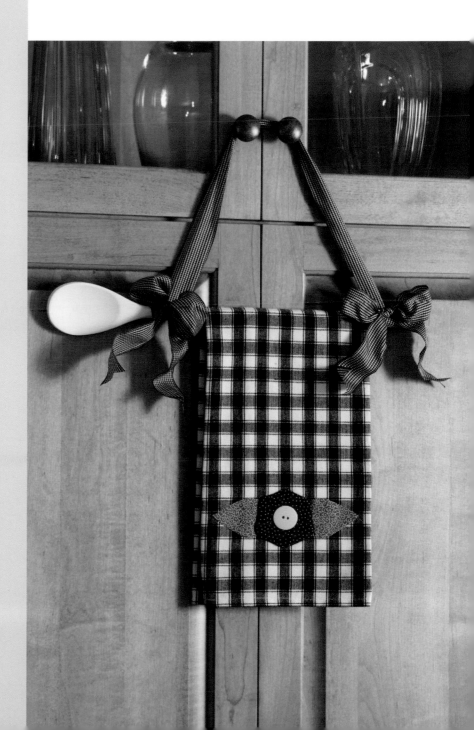

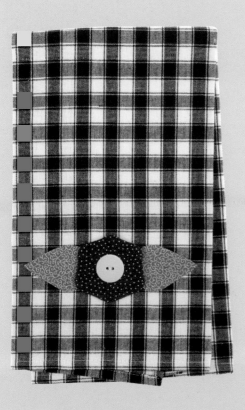

1. Prepare the two green fabric leaf appliqués using either of the Freezer Paper methods on page 13 and the leaf pattern.

2. Prepare the flower appliqué using the Fleece Padding technique on page 11 and the flower pattern.

3. Pin the leaf appliqués on the front of the tea towel about 3" up from the bottom of the towel and 1¾" apart.

4. Use an invisible appliqué stitch to sew the leaves in place.

5. Sew the flower between the leaves, overlapping the edge of each leaf.

6. Sew the yellow button to the center of the flower, sewing through the towel front.

7. Paint the spoon white, re-coating as necessary for good coverage.

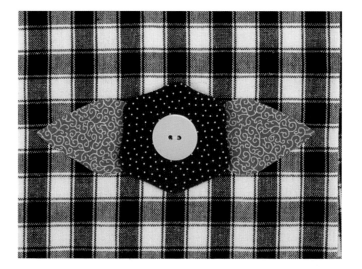

8. Cut the ribbon into three 24" lengths.

9. Tie two of the lengths into bows and set aside. The remaining ribbon is the hanger for the spoon.

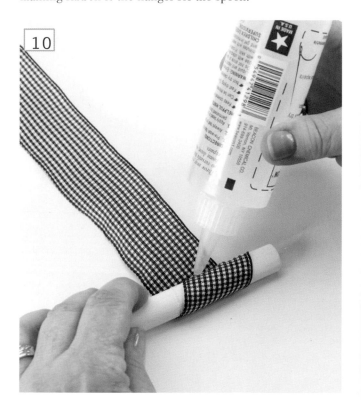

10. To attach the ribbon to the spoon, wrap one ribbon end around the end of the spoon at an angle and glue in place. Wrap and glue the other ribbon end next to the spoon end. Be sure that the ribbon is not twisted in the center before gluing the other end.

11

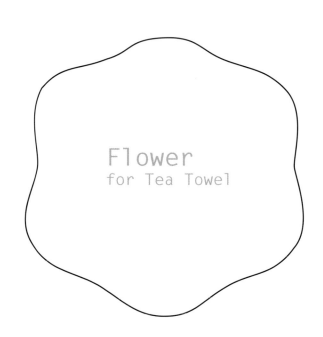

Flower
for Tea Towel

**11.** Glue a ribbon bow to each end of the spoon hanger, covering the wrapped ends.

**12.** Fold the towel so the appliqués are centered and hang the towel over the middle of the spoon handle.

Leaf
for Tea Towel

# "Life is a Picnic"

*Gather all of the traditional picnic food together and have a party—but this time, the ants are invited. This collection includes a vinyl tablecloth with a column of marching ants stamped down each side. The mini quilt on the large basket will let your guests know that "Life is a Picnic." The small basket has a reversible ruffled liner and echoes the ant theme. The denim place mat with pocket napkin holder adds to the comfortable, casual feel.*

## FABRIC SELECTION

This set is made with red, white and blue fabric—prints, denim and vinyl—all to suggest a fun, easy-going style. Any combination of bright colors would be appropriate for outdoor dining in the summer. A green-and-white checked tablecloth with fabric accessories in the sunflower colors of yellow, orange and red would be very pretty. Instead of a jeans pocket, tie raffia around the napkin and add a pot of real sunflowers for a centerpiece.

# Stamped Tablecloth
Finished size: 44" x 88" (to fit a 28" x 72" picnic table)

## MATERIALS

Fabric:
- ◇ 2½ yd. red-and-white checked vinyl cloth

Outdoor gloss acrylic paint:
- ◇ Black
- ◇ White

White or red sewing thread

1¾" x ¾" ant rubber stamp

Permanent black medium-point marker

Rubbing alcohol

Paper towels

Disposable plate (for palette)

Small foam brush

Toothpick

*A checked vinyl tablecloth is practical and cheery, but adding some rubber-stamped characters to the sides really makes it stand out. Children would enjoy helping with this project!*

1. Measure the picnic table to be covered. Cut a piece of vinyl 8½" larger on all sides for the overhang (the tablecloth shown was cut 45" x 89" and fits a 28" x 72" table after ½" hem is sewn around the edges).

2. Measure up about 11" from the edge along one long side. Wet a paper towel with rubbing alcohol and clean a 2" section down the length of the cloth where the stamp will be positioned. This helps the paint adhere better to the vinyl. Repeat on the other long side.

3. Pour a puddle of black paint on the plate and use the foam brush to apply the paint evenly to the stamp.

4. Starting at one end of the tablecloth, press the stamp in place and lift it straight up. Re-apply paint for each stamping. Vary the position slightly with each figure, having some angling up or down, all about 1½" apart. Repeat the process along the other long side. Let dry.

5. When the paint has dried, use the permanent marker to draw a curving dashed line between the ants.

6. To make the eye on each ant, dip a toothpick in white paint and touch it to the ant's head. Let dry.

7. If desired, fold under ½" hem along all the edges and sew in place.

## TIP

Use a scrap of the vinyl remnant to practice a few stamps before starting the tablecloth. Here's a tip to help you get all the ants stamped right-side up: Place a sticker with a definite top and bottom, such as an ad-dress label, on the back of the stamp. If your sticker is upside down, so is your stamp!

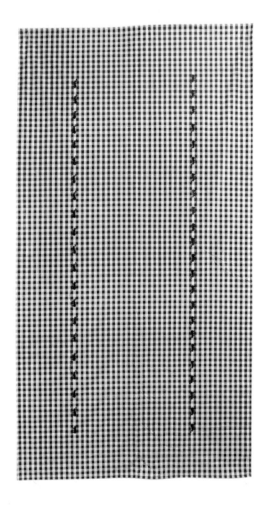

# Place Mat and Napkin
Finished size: 17" x 13" place mat, 16" square napkin

## MATERIALS

(for one place mat and one napkin)

Fabric:
- ½ yd. blue-and-white denim print
- Fat quarter red-and-white check

17½" x 13½" piece of batting

2 yd. red jumbo rick rack

Small denim pocket cut from an old pair of jeans (model is 3½" across at the top)

1 yd. red grosgrain ribbon, 1" wide

Matching sewing threads

Fray preventative

Permanent fabric adhesive

## CUTTING INSTRUCTIONS

From the blue-and-white denim print, cut:
- Two 17½" x 13½" place mat centers

From the red-and-white check, cut:
- One 16" square

*A patterned denim and a cheerful red check team up with a recycled jeans pocket to make this place mat and napkin set. The place mat can be folded, tied with a ribbon and arranged in a basket for a buffet setting.*

# PLACE MAT INSTRUCTIONS

1. Starting on one long side of a denim place mat center, place the rick rack along the edge on the right side so the midpoint of the trim lies on the ¼" seam allowance.

2. Baste the rick rack all around the place mat, overlapping about ½" at the end.

3. Trim off the excess and apply fray preventative to the cut ends.

4. Machine stitch the rick rack in place.

5. Place the other denim place mat center over the one with rick rack, right sides together. Layer these on top of the batting and pin.

6. Sew all around the place mat, leaving a 5" opening along one side.

7. Clip the corners and turn right-side out.

8. Fold in the seam allowance on the opening, leaving the rick rack edge pointing outward and hand stitch the opening closed with small invisible stitches. Press well.

9. Trim closely around the edges of the denim pocket.

11. Fold the napkin and tuck it into the top of the pocket or pull it through so it extends at the top and bottom of the pocket holder.

10. Hold the pocket in place at the left side of the place mat and cup it slightly so there is more room to insert a napkin. Apply glue to the upper corners of the pocket and down each side about 2" and press the pocket to the place mat. Leave the bottom free. Let dry.

# NAPKIN INSTRUCTIONS

1. Make a fringed napkin with the red-and-white check square following the Fringed Edge instructions on page 15.

# "Life is a Picnic" Mini Quilt Basket

Finished size: 5½" square mini quilt

*Stitching up a mini quilt and putting it on a ribbon to tie around a basket is such a simple way to decorate a table setting. This basket is large enough to hold plates and folded and tied place mats.*

## MATERIALS

Fabric:
◇ Scrap of white solid for the embroidered panel
◇ Scrap of red-and-white print for the inner border
◇ Scrap of blue denim print for the outer border and backing

Basket (model is 10½" x 7", not including the handle)

6" square batting

Black embroidery floss

5 feet blue grosgrain ribbon, 1" wide

4 blue buttons, ¾" diameter

Matching sewing threads

Fade-out pen

Small embroidery hoop

Embroidery needle

Quilting needle

Quilting thread for hand quilting:
◇ White
◇ Red

Patterns:
◇ Life is a Picnic, page 37

## CUTTING INSTRUCTIONS

From the white solid, cut:
◇ One 8½" square panel

From the red-and-white print, cut:
◇ Two ¾" x 3½" inner border strips
◇ Two ¾" x 4" inner border strips

From the blue denim print, cut:
◇ Two 1½" x 4" outer border strips
◇ Two 1½" x 6" outer border strips
◇ One 6" square backing

1. Transfer the words "Life is a Picnic" onto the center of the white square panel with the fade-out pen.

2. Place the panel in the embroidery hoop.

3. Using two strands of black embroidery floss, backstitch over the lines of the letters. Make a French knot for each dot.

4. Remove the fabric from the hoop, but do not press until the marker completely fades away (applying a little water with a cotton-tip swab will speed it up).

5. Trim the embroidered fabric to a 3½" square.

6. Sew the 3½" inner border strips to the sides of the embroidered square; press the seams outward.

7. Sew the 4" inner border strips to the top and bottom of the embroidered square; press the seams outward.

8. Sew the 4" outer border strips to the sides of the bordered square; press the seams outward.

9. Sew the 6" outer border strips to the top and bottom of the embroidered square; press the seams outward.

10. To finish, follow the Self Binding instructions on page 10.

11. To finish, quilt by "stitching in the ditch" between the red border and the stitched center with white quilting thread and between the two borders with red quilting thread.

12. Lay the ribbon out flat in front of you (horizontally). Place the mini quilt on the ribbon so the top edges are even and the ribbon extends about 18" on the right side and 36" on the left.

13. Place a button at each top corner of the mini quilt. Sew each button to the mini quilt and through the ribbon.

14. Sew the remaining two buttons to the bottom corners of the quilt.

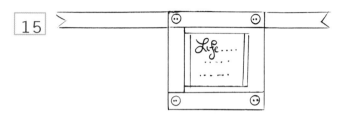

15

15. Hold the ribbon with the quilt centered in front. Wrap the long end around the basket and tie the ends in a bow at the right of the quilt.

16. Trim the ribbon ends in a V-cut.

# Basket with Reversible Ruffled Liner
Finished size: 13" x 14½" liner

## MATERIALS

Fabric:
- ◇ Fat quarter blue denim print
- ◇ Fat quarter red-and-white print
- ◇ ¼ yd. red-and-white check

Basket
- ◇ *Note:* Model is 6" x 5" x 4½"; adjust liner size for a different size basket.

Matching sewing threads

Black button, ⅜" diameter

2 black buttons, ⁹⁄₁₆" diameter

8" length of 24-gauge black wire

Permanent fabric adhesive

Wire cutters

## CUTTING INSTRUCTIONS

From the blue denim print, cut:
- ◇ One 13½" x 15" rectangle

From the red-and-white print, cut:
- ◇ One 13½" x 15" lining

From the red-and-white check, cut:
- ◇ Three 2½" x 44" strips

*This ruffled liner will add a touch of class to your picnic. Use it in a basket to organize your flatware or by itself as a bread liner. Make the basket part of your picnic set with a button ant, echoing the theme of the tablecloth.*

1. Sew the red-and-white check strips together at the short ends to make a continuous circle, 130½" around.

2. Fold and press the strip in half lengthwise, wrong sides together.

3. Sew two rows of machine gathering ⅜" and ¼" from the raw edges, sewing through both layers. Do not backstitch at the ends.

4. To gather the ruffle, pull on the two bobbin threads, carefully spreading the gathers down the length of half of the ruffle. Start at the other end to gather the remaining half.

5. When the ruffle is looking like it may fit around the denim rectangle, begin to pin the ruffle along the edge of the denim, on the right side, matching the raw edges. Add or release gathers until the ruffle fits exactly and then tie off the threads and clip them. Push the gathers around until they are evenly distributed.

## BUTTON ANT INSTRUCTIONS

1. Use the wire cutters to cut the wire into four 2" lengths.

2. Fold three of these pieces in half for legs.

3. Curl one end of the remaining wire for antenna.

4. Glue the legs to the basket.

5. Glue the two larger buttons over the top of the legs for a body.

6. Glue the smaller button to the basket for a head with the straight end of the antenna glued under the edge of the button.

6. Hand or machine baste the ruffle to the denim rectangle.

7. Place the red-and-white print lining on the ruffled denim, right sides together, and pin.

8. Stitch all around with a ⅜" seam, leaving a 4" opening along one side for turning.

9. Clip the corners and turn the liner right-side out; press.

10. Fold in the seam allowance on the opening and hand sew it closed with small stitches. Topstitch ¼" from the seam, if desired.

# Autumn Leaves

When the air gets crisp and the days grow shorter, the leaves start going through their annual extravaganza, turning rich hues of gold, green and red. This vibrant palette of colors inspires a variety of projects for the dining room and kitchen.

This collection dramatically shows the impact that fabric patterns and textures have on design. Combining a variety of prints, including some with a polished finish or metallic highlights, produces an elegant table runner, reversible napkins and beaded napkin holders—just the look for special occasion dining. Using plaid homespun and osnaburg fabrics gives place mats, coasters and an appliance cover a casual, comfortable look for the kitchen.

## FABRIC SELECTION

I chose a variety of prints that included a full range of fall colors plus an accent color (in this case, the accent color is just a touch of purple to liven up the collection). A few fabrics with a shiny finish or gold and copper highlights add to the mood, especially in the glow of candlelight. The metallic floss on the appliqués and the glass beads on the napkin holders accentuate the ambience.

# Quilted Table Runner
Finished size: 12½" x 42½"

## MATERIALS

**Fabric:**
- ¼ yd. polished ivory for patchwork center
- 8-10 fat quarters in assorted fall colors, including a few with metallic highlights for the patchwork border
- 1¼ yd. copper for the backing, binding and patchwork

15" x 45" batting

Metallic copper embroidery floss

Matching sewing threads

Ecru quilting thread for hand quilting

Fusible web

Quilting needle and hoop

**Patterns:**
- Leaf, page 42

## CUTTING INSTRUCTIONS

From the ivory, cut:
- 16 squares (3½")

From the assorted fat quarter prints, cut:
- 40 squares (3½")

From the copper, cut:
- One 15" x 45" backing
- Three 2¼" x 40" binding strips

*Note:* It is a good idea to cut a few extra colored squares when combining so many prints, because it's often necessary to switch fabrics back and forth until you achieve a good mix. Be sure to leave enough print fabric for 10 leaf appliqués.

*This elegant table dressing uses simple patchwork squares in a variety of prints and a shimmery ivory background fabric embellished with appliqué leaves and simple quilting. Details like the blanket stitch with metallic copper embroidery floss and a double binding in a coppery fabric finish the runner.*

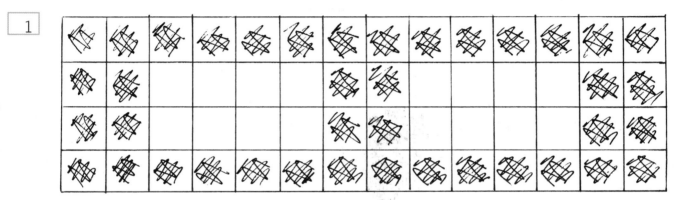

1. Following the diagram, arrange the ivory squares into two blocks that are four squares across and two squares down. Place colored squares all around the ivory sections. Try to keep the colors balanced and avoid having matching fabrics adjacent to each other.

2. Sew the squares together in each long row. Press the seam allowance in one direction, alternating the direction of each row.

3. Join the rows together, following the diagram.

4. Trace five leaves onto the paper side of the fusible web and then reverse the pattern and trace an additional five leaves. Refer to Fusible Appliqué on page 12 to prepare the appliqués using the assortment of the fall-color prints.

5. Position five leaves on each ivory panel, referring to the photo for placement. Notice that several of the leaves overlap slightly and that the last leaf on each side overlaps the border. Fuse the appliqués in place.

6. Use two strands of metallic copper embroidery floss to blanket stitch around each leaf.

7. Layer the backing, batting and pieced top, and baste through all the layers as described in Backing, Batting and Basting on page 9. The backing and batting are larger than the top and will be trimmed after quilting.

8. Quilt "in the ditch" on all seams.

9. Trim the backing and batting even with the top. Press thoroughly.

10. Refer to Applied Binding on page 10 to prepare the binding strips and sew them to the runner.

Leaf
for Table Runner

# Bordered Reversible Napkin with Beaded Napkin Holder

Finished size: 16" square

## MATERIALS

(for one napkin and napkin holder)

Fabric:
- ◇ Fat quarter ivory
- ◇ ⅔ yd. colored print
- ◇ Scrap of copper
- ◇ Scrap of fleece

Shank button, 1⅜" diameter

28" length of 24-gauge wire

Copper- and gold-colored glass rocaille beads

30" copper wired-edge ribbon, 2" wide

Permanent fabric adhesive

Wire cutters

## CUTTING INSTRUCTIONS

From the ivory, cut:
- ◇ One 16" square

From the colored print, cut:
- ◇ One 20" square

From the copper, cut:
- ◇ One 3" diameter circle

From the fleece, cut:
- ◇ One 1⅜" diameter circle

*This luxurious napkin is made using two fabrics from the table runner—the ivory and a multicolored print with metallic highlights. Dress up your napkin and add sparkle to your table with the metallic wire-edged ribbon and beaded leaves.*

1. Glue the fleece circle to the top of the button.

2. To cover the button, finger press ⅛" hem around the edge of the fabric circle and hand sew a gathering stitch all around, close to the fold, using a doubled length of matching thread.

3. Place the fleece-covered side of the button in the center of the circle. Pull the thread to gather the fabric snugly around the shank of the button; knot and clip the thread.

4. Cut the wire in half; each 14" piece will make one beaded leaf.

5. Fold 2" of each wire up to prevent the beads from slipping off and string enough beads of one color on each wire to make a 10" beaded section.

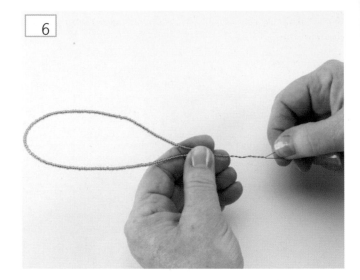

6. Twist the wire ends tightly together to hold the beads in place.

7. Form the top loop of the leaf at the center of the beaded section with your fingers. Gently shape two more loops on each side, forming a leaf. Repeat to make a second leaf.

8. Clip the wire ends to ½" and push them through the shank of the button.

9. To cover the wire and hold it in place, pull the fabric gathers over the wires and secure with several small stitches.

10. Gather the ribbon with your fingers about 12" from one end; sew the button shank to the ribbon at this position.

11. Wrap the longer end of ribbon around the folded napkin and tie the ends in a bow, right next to the button.

## NAPKIN INSTRUCTIONS

1. Refer to Reversible Napkin with Border on page 15 to make the napkin with the two fabric squares.

# Kitchen Set

Simply by changing the fabric selection, especially in pattern and texture, the same pairing of patchwork squares and appliquéd leaves takes on a totally different look. The osnaburg solids and plaid homespuns in the place mat, napkin, coasters and toaster cover combine to inspire a casual and comfortable mood.

Black embroidery floss for the blanket stitching and the "big stitch" quilting contribute to the informal setting. The leaf pattern is the same size as in the table runner, but is modified slightly to be more stylized.

## FABRIC SELECTION

I used a variety of plaids in the fall color palette. Natural and tea-bag osnaburg add more visual texture. The accent color in this mix is black, used as a binding for the place mat and in the appliqué and quilting stitches.

# Toaster Cover

Finished size: 12" x 10" (to fit a standard two-slice toaster)

## MATERIALS

Fabric:

◇ ½ yd. natural osnaburg for the appliqué squares and side panel
◇ 1 yd. plaid homespun for the back, lining and bias binding
◇ Scraps of 6 assorted plaid homespuns for the squares and leaves
◇ ⅛ yd. tea-bag osnaburg
◇ ½ yd. fleece

Black embroidery floss

Large piece of paper or double sheet of newspaper for the pattern

Dinner plate for the pattern

Patterns:

◇ Leaf, page 51

## CUTTING INSTRUCTIONS

From the natural osnaburg, cut:

◇ Three 4½" squares
◇ One 8" x 34½" strip

From the plaid homespun, cut:

◇ One 8" x 34½" strip
◇ Two 2¼" x 36" bias binding strips
◇ *Note:* Be sure to leave enough fabric for three patterns (see Step 9).

From the assorted plaid homespuns, cut:

◇ Three 4½" squares
◇ *Note:* You will use the remaining three plaids for the leaf appliqués.

From the tea-bag osnaburg, cut:

◇ One 2½" x 12" strip

From the fleece, cut:

◇ One 8" x 34½" strip
◇ *Note:* Be sure to leave enough fabric for two patterns (see Step 9).

*An appliance cover is a crafty way to keep appliances clean and handy for daily use and decorate the kitchen at the same time.*

*This cover repeats the leaf and patchwork square designs and is backed and lined with plaid. The same plaid fabric is used for the bias binding.*

1. Trace three leaves on the paper side of the fusible web. Refer to Fusible Appliqués on page 12 to prepare the appliqués on the remaining three plaid fabrics.

2. Position each leaf diagonally on an osnaburg square and fuse in place.

3. Use two strands of black embroidery floss to blanket stitch around each leaf.

4. Pin and sew two rows of three squares together, alternating the appliquéd and plaid squares, as shown in the illustration. Press the seams in different directions for each row.

5. Sew the two rows together, matching the seam lines.

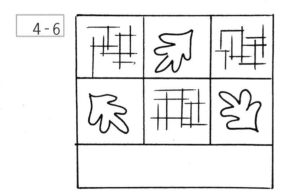

6. Sew the tea-bag strip to the bottom of the squares.

7. To make the pattern for the toaster cover front and back, cut a piece of paper 12" x 10½". Fold the paper in half so it measures 6" x 10½".

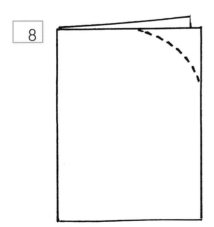

8. Use a dinner plate to round off the top corners on the side without the fold.

9. Use the pattern to cut three pieces from the plaid for the back and the lining, two from the fleece and to cut the curve at the top corners of the pieced front.

10. Baste the fleece strip to the wrong side of each front and back section and to the side section.

11. With the right sides together, pin the lining to each front and back piece. Stitch along the straight bottom edge. Press the seam allowance toward the lining.

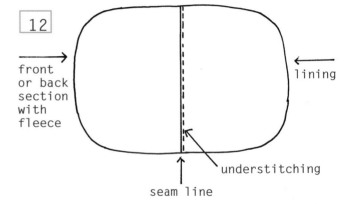

12. Understitch by sewing very close to the seam, through the lining and the seam allowance. This helps the lining stay in place and makes the fold crisper and neater.

13. Turn the lining to the wrong side, matching the raw edges. Baste the layers together close to the raw edges.

14. To finish the front of the cover, use two strands of black embroidery floss to "big stitch" quilt diagonally through each plaid square and around each leaf. "Big stitch" quilt ¼" from the long seams on the bottom strip.

15. Pin the lining to the side section at each short end, right sides together. Stitch the seam and press the seam allowance toward the lining at both ends.

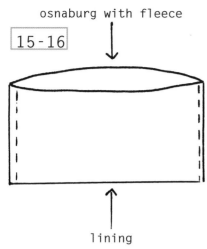

osnaburg with fleece

15-16

↑ lining

**16.** Understitch each seam, as for the front and back.

**17.** Turn the lining to the wrong side, matching the raw edges. Baste the layers together, close to the raw edge.

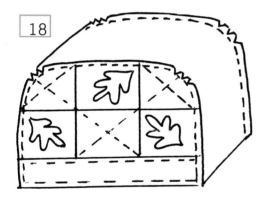

18

**18.** Pin the front section to one long edge of the side section, with the lining sides together. Repeat with the back section and the remaining long edge of the side section. Clip the seam allowance as necessary on the curves (the seams are on the outside of the cover).

**19.** To cover and finish the seams, fold each bias binding strip in half lengthwise, wrong sides together, and press.

**20.** Pin one binding piece to the front of the toaster cover, matching the raw edges of the binding to the raw edges of the seam. Extend the binding ½" beyond the bottom edge on both sides of the cover; trim off any excess binding.

**21.** Stitch the binding in place, sewing over the existing seam line.

**22.** To finish the bottom edges, fold the extending end of the binding back over the seam allowance; press.

**23.** Finish the binding by folding it over the seam and hand stitching it in place.

24

**24.** Fold in the bottom edge of the binding and make a few stitches to close it in.

## MAKING COVERS FOR OTHER KITCHEN APPLIANCES

Use these same steps to make covers for larger toasters, coffee makers or mixers. Measure the height and width of the appliance and add at least 1". This will give you the pattern for the front and back of the cover. Add more patchwork at the bottom or sides, or insert a coordinating strip so the pieced front fits the pattern measurements. For the width of the side section, measure the depth of the appliance, taking into account electric cords and knobs. To measure the length needed for the side section, use a cloth tape measure and carefully lay it against the sides and top of the cover front.

# Place Mat

**Finished size: 16" x 13"**

## MATERIALS

(for one place mat)

Fabric:
- ¼ yd. natural osnaburg for the top
- ¼ yd. tea-bag osnaburg for the top
- ½ yd. black plaid for the binding and backing
- Scraps of assorted plaid homespuns in fall colors for patchwork squares and leaves

16" x 13" batting

Black embroidery floss

Fusible web

Matching sewing thread

Embroidery needle

Patterns:
- Leaf, page 51

## CUTTING INSTRUCTIONS

From the natural osnaburg, cut:
- One 5" x 13" strip

From the tea-bag osnaburg, cut:
- One 9" x 13" panel

From the black plaid, cut:
- One 16" x 13" backing
- Two 2" x 32" binding strips

From the assorted plaids, cut:
- Four 4" squares
- *Note:* Be sure to leave enough fabric for three leaf appliqués.

*This place mat has a band of quilted patchwork plaids on one side and blanket-stitched leaves falling down the other side. The look is casual and perfect for the kitchen table or counter.*

Use ½" seam allowance for this project.

1. Sew the four 4" plaid squares together in a row; press the seams in one direction.

2. Sew the patchwork row to the left side of the tea-bag osnaburg panel.

3. Sew the natural osnaburg strip to the right side of the tea-bag osnaburg panel.

4. Trace three leaves on the paper side of the fusible web. Refer to Fusible Appliqué on page 12 to prepare the appliqués on three assorted plaid fabrics.

**Leaf**
for Toaster Cover,
Place Mat and
Coaster

5. Position the leaves down the center of the natural osnaburg strip, angling each leaf slightly, as shown in the photo. Fuse the appliqués in place.

6. Use two strands of black embroidery floss to blanket stitch around each leaf appliqué.

7. Layer and baste the backing, batting and pieced top as described in Backing, Batting and Basting on page 9.

8. Refer to Applied Binding on page 10 to prepare the binding and sew it to the edges of the place mat.

9. Finish the place mat with "big stitch" quilting (a larger running stitch). Use two strands of black floss to quilt diagonally through the pieced squares, around each leaf and ¼" from the seams on the center panel.

# Napkin
Finished size: 16" square

## MATERIALS

Fabric:
- ◇ Fat quarter light-colored homespun

Matching sewing thread

## CUTTING INSTRUCTIONS

From the light-colored homespun, cut:
- ◇ One 17" square

*Finish the set with a simple napkin made from a coordinating plaid homespun. Use a grapevine wreath as a napkin holder to complete the look.*

1. Press ¼" hem all around the 17" square.

2. Fold the hem again so it is doubled and press well.

3. Use a few pins to hold the hem in place and stitch all around.

## NAPKIN HOLDER IDEAS

I used a simple miniature grapevine wreath for an informal napkin holder for this set. Other simple ideas to spruce up a napkin include pushing it through a cookie cutter or painted wood curtain ring; or tying it with raffia, ribbon or a torn strip of fabric.

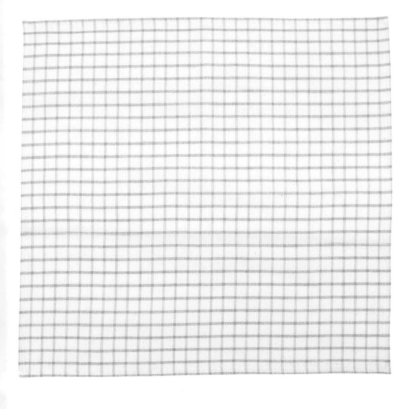

# Coasters
Finished size: 5" square

## MATERIALS
(for one coaster)

Fabric:
- ◇ Scrap of tea-bag osnaburg
- ◇ Scrap of plaid homespun for leaf, border and backing
- ◇ Scrap of fleece

Black embroidery floss

Matching sewing threads

Fusible web

Patterns:
- ◇ Leaf, page 51

## CUTTING INSTRUCTIONS

From the tea-bag osnaburg, cut:
- ◇ One 4½" square top

From the plaid homespun, cut:
- ◇ One 5½" square backing
- ◇ Two 1" x 4½" strips
- ◇ Two 1" x 5½" strips

From the fleece, cut:
- ◇ One 5½" square

*These leaf coasters are quick, easy and look great in a variety of plaids.*

1. Trace one leaf onto the paper side of the fusible web. Refer to Fusible Appliqués on page 12 to prepare the appliqué on the plaid fabric.

2. Fuse the leaf appliqué to the center of the osnaburg square.

3. Use two strands of black embroidery floss to blanket stitch around the leaf.

4. Sew the 4½" strips to the top and bottom of the osnaburg; press seams outward.

5. Sew the 5½" strips to the sides; press the seams outward.

6. Place the top and backing right sides together, and pin to the fleece square. Sew all around, leaving a 2" opening on one side.

7. Clip corners and trim the fleece close to the seam. Turn right-side out through the opening. Fold in the seam allowance on the opening and hand sew the opening closed.

8. Use two strands of floss to "big stitch" quilt near the seam line on the osnaburg.

# Tea Party

When I think of a tea party, I think of colors like pink and fresh white, of flowers and ribbons. This set has all that and more. Fashion a tea cozy from patchworked fabrics with a strip of silk ribbon embroidered flowers.

The reversible napkin is practical but sweet when paired with a ribbon rose napkin holder. The place mat and apron bib echo the floral theme with simple quilted borders around a floral center. A sweet place card with a single silk ribbon flower and a few buttons finish the table.

## FABRIC SELECTION

The pretty pastels and florals definitely contribute to a lovely, feminine look, just right for a tea party. Having a variety of fabric (patterns and colors) makes the collection more interesting. This same group could be sewn in bright colors to accompany a more modern pottery tea set.

# Silk Ribbon Embroidered Tea Cozy

Finished size: 14" x 14½"

## MATERIALS

Fabric:
- ◇ Scraps of assorted fabrics in rose, yellow, soft green, lavender, florals, dots and plaids for patchwork
- ◇ ⅜ yd. coordinating print for the lining
- ◇ ¼ yd. white solid for the embroidered panel

Silk ribbon:
- ◇ 1 package 4mm light blue
- ◇ 1 package 4mm soft green
- ◇ 1 package 7mm lavender
- ◇ 1 package 7mm pale gold
- ◇ 2 packages 13mm variegated rose

Embroidery floss:
- ◇ Soft green
- ◇ Rose

30" x 24" batting

1 yd. white double-fold bias tape

1 yd. white maxi piping

36 white buttons, ½" diameter

Matching sewing threads

15" x 12" sheet of paper

Standard-size dinner plate

Chenille or tapestry needle for silk ribbon embroidery

Embroidery needle

Embroidery hoop

Fade-out pen

Zipper foot for sewing machine

Patterns:
- ◇ Flower Vine, page 68

## CUTTING INSTRUCTIONS

From the white solid, cut:
- ◇ One 16" x 8" strip

From the assorted fabric scraps, cut:
- ◇ 54 squares (3")

*Pull out your stash of pretty fabric scraps for this project—the more, the better. The silk ribbon embroidery is a charming adornment for the tea cozy and very easy to do. The buttons hold the layers together and add another dimensional embellishment.*

1. To make the silk ribbon embroidered strip for the tea cozy, use the fade-out pen to transfer the flower vine pattern to the center of the white fabric strip.

2. Place the fabric in the embroidery hoop. Using two strands of green floss, stem stitch the vine.

3. Refer to the Silk Ribbon Stitches diagrams on pages 59-60. Use the pink floss to stitch the spokes for the five spider web roses. Thread the chenille needle with the variegated ribbon and weave around the spokes, keeping the ribbon somewhat loose and letting it twist to make a soft rose.

4. Follow the pattern and the photo to embroider the following:
   ◊ Two blue flowers with the lazy daisy stitch
   ◊ Two lavender and two pale gold flowers with the Japanese ribbon stitch
   ◊ Three green lazy daisy stitches at each end of the vine and on each side of the center rose
   ◊ Green leaves along the vine and around the flowers with the Japanese Ribbon stitch
   ◊ Gold French knot at the center of the blue flowers
   ◊ Green French knot at the base of the three leaves at the ends of the vine

5. Remove the fabric from the embroidery hoop and carefully press out the hoop marks without disturbing the embroidery.

6. Cut this fabric into a 15½" x 3" strip with the embroidered section in the center.

7. Lay out the assorted 3" squares on your work surface in rows of six squares, keeping a good mixture of colors and patterns. You will need four rows for the front of the cozy and five rows for the back.

8. When you are satisfied with the arrangement, pin the squares together in each row and sew. Press the seams in opposing directions for each row.

9. Sew each row together, inserting the embroidered strip between rows 3 and 4 on the front (the strip will be right above the bottom row).

10. To make a pattern for the cozy, fold the paper in half so it measures 7½" x 12". Place the dinner plate at the top edge of the paper and trace the curve onto the paper on the unfolded corners.

11. Cut out the pattern and place it on the pieced front; pin and cut out.

12. Use the pattern to cut one back, two lining pieces and two batting pieces.

13. Layer one lining right-side down, one batting piece on top, and the front of the cozy right-side up. Pin the layers together and machine baste all around, about ³⁄₁₆" from the edge. Repeat with the cozy back.

14. Pin piping around the sides and top of the cozy front, with the raw edge of the piping even with the raw edge of the cozy. Using a zipper foot, machine baste close to the cord. Trim away any excess piping.

15. Pin the cozy front and back right sides together and sew the sides and top.

16. Finish the seam by either sewing a close zigzag stitch on the machine or hand sewing a small blanket stitch to cover the raw edges.

17. Unfold the bias tape and fold in a ¼" hem at one end. Pin the tape along the bottom outside edge of the cozy, matching the raw edges of the tape and the fabric. Overlap the ends.

18. Sew the bias tape to the fabric along the fold of the tape.

19. Fold the tape over the bottom edge of the cozy and hand stitch it to the inside.

20. Sew a white button to each corner of a patchwork square on the front and the back of the cozy. *Note:* Slip a magazine or a piece of cardboard inside the cozy to prevent sewing through to the opposite side.

## TIP

Silk ribbon can be washed with warm water and a mild soap. Lay it flat to dry and iron from the back. Place the embroidery face down on a terrycloth towel and press gently with a warm iron so as not to flatten the stitches.

## MATERIALS

Silk ribbon
Fabric
Chenille needle (long eye, sharp point)
Small sharp scissors
Fade-out pen to draw the pattern
Embroidery hoop to hold the fabric taut
Embroidery floss and embroidery needle for some steps
Iron to press the ribbons if necessary

*Making simple embroidery stitches with silk ribbon adds a lushness and soft beauty to any project it adorns. Practice the stitches first if you wish, but it is important to know that this technique is very forgiving. Each stitch does not have to be a perfect copy of the last. The beauty is in the color, sheen and softness of the ribbon.*

## Beginning Knot

*Silk ribbon embroidery starts with a soft, flat knot that supports the ribbon without the bulk of a traditional knot.*

Thread a length of ribbon (about 20") through the eye of the needle. To make a flat knot, fold the end of the ribbon down about ¼" and pierce the fold with the point of the needle. Pull that fold down the needle and down the ribbon until it forms a small soft knot at the end.

## Japanese Ribbon Stitch

*This is probably the most used and versatile stitch in silk ribbon embroidery and is also very easy.*

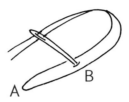

Bring the ribbon up through the fabric (A) and lay it smooth on the fabric in the direction of the stitch. Use the needle point to pierce the ribbon at the end of the desired stitch (B). Pull the ribbon through slowly and carefully so the end of the stitch will form a rolled edge on each side of the point.

## Ending Knot

*The ending knot is similar to the knot made when hand sewing.*

Bring the needle to the back of the fabric. Turn the needle and slip the eye under the back of a previously worked stitch. Pull the needle through the ribbon loop very gently until the knot is tight. Cut off the ribbon, leaving a small tail. Sometimes it is a good idea to tack these tails down with a few small stitches with thread or floss if they are not holding tight.

# French Knot

*This dimensional stitch is created by wrapping the ribbon around the needle. It is used often for flower centers, small flowers and flower clusters.*

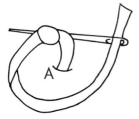

Bring the ribbon up through the fabric (A). Tip the needle parallel to the fabric and wrap the ribbon around the needle two times. Hold the ribbon so it stays snug and turn the needle back down and insert the point back into the fabric very close to where the ribbon came up. Carefully pull the ribbon down with the needle, leaving a soft knot on the fabric.

# Lazy Daisy Stitch

*This is a single chain stitch and is often used for leaves and flower petals.*

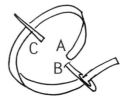

Bring the ribbon up through the fabric (A). Holding the ribbon down with the thumb of the hand not holding the needle, insert the needle back into the fabric (B) very close to the point where the ribbon came up. In the same motion, bring the needle back up at the desired end point of the stitch (C). Pull the ribbon so it forms a smooth loop. Secure the top of the loop by making a small stitch over the top. Do not pull this stitch too snug; it looks best when it is left soft and full.

# Spider Web Rose

*This spectacular stitch gets its name from the web-like stitching that provides a base for weaving the ribbon around and around to form the rose. It is surprisingly easy to do and very sturdy.*

Use thread or floss in a color that matches the ribbon. Follow the pattern and make five straight stitches from the center of the circle out to the edge. Knot and clip the thread. Bring the ribbon up through the fabric at the center of the circle, right beside a thread spoke (A). Remaining on the surface of the fabric, weave the ribbon over and under the spokes, which will alternate as you go round and round. Keep the ribbon a little loose and soft and allow it to twist. When the rose is as full and large as you want, insert the needle to the back of the fabric to knot off.

Lazy daisy flower with French knot center and Japanese ribbon stitch flower and leaves.

Spider web rose and lazy daisy leaves.

# Quilted Place Mat
Finished size: 16½" x 12½"

## MATERIALS

(for one place mat)

Fabric:
- ¼ yd. pink floral for the center
- ⅛ yd. blue floral for the inner border
- ⅜ yd. pink plaid for the outer border and backing

17" x 13" batting

Matching sewing threads

Quilting needle

White quilting thread for hand quilting

## CUTTING INSTRUCTIONS

From the pink floral, cut:
- One 11" x 7" center

From the blue floral, cut:
- Two 1¼" x 7" inner border strips
- Two 1¼" x 12½" inner border strips

From the pink plaid, cut:
- One 17" x 13" backing
- Two 2¾" x 8½" outer border strips
- Two 2¾" x 17" outer border strips

## INSTRUCTIONS

1. Sew the 7" blue inner border strips to each side of the pink floral center; press the seams outward.

2. Sew the 12½" blue inner border strips to the top and bottom of the pink floral center; press the seams outward.

3. Sew the 8½" plaid outer border strips to each side of the bordered panel; press the seams outward.

4. Sew the 17" plaid outer border strips to the top and bottom of the bordered panel; press the seams outward.

5. Add the batting and finish the construction of the place mat using the Self-Binding technique on page 10.

6. Quilt by stitching "in the ditch" between the center panel and the blue border, and again between the two borders.

*This place mat is a simple center panel with a striking rose motif and two strongly contrasting borders—a blue floral and a pink plaid. I used a high-loft batting to give it a soft puffy look.*

# Place Card

Finished size: 4½" x 3½"

## MATERIALS

(for one place card)

Patterned cardstock or fabric swatch and a color copier

White cardstock for name

Silk ribbon:
- ◇ 4mm pink
- ◇ 4mm pale gold
- ◇ 4mm soft green

Chenille needle

4 pink buttons, ⅜" diameter

Black calligraphy pen or computer font

Bone folder

Permanent fabric adhesive

*A place card is a special touch that each guest will appreciate. Make your own patterned background by copying fabric onto cardstock, then add a silk ribbon flower for a simple but unique embellishment.*

# INSTRUCTIONS

1. If you wish to make your own patterned cardstock that will coordinate with your table setting, choose a small-print fabric about 8" x 11" and press it to remove any wrinkles. Lay it flat on the scanner of the color copy printer, print side down, and copy it onto a piece of white cardstock.

2. Cut a 4½" x 7" rectangle from the patterned cardstock and fold it in half crosswise. Use a bone folder to make a sharp crease.

3. Write the name on a 3¼" x 1¾" piece of white cardstock or use a fancy computer font to print the name on white cardstock and trim it to that size. The name should be on the right ⅔ of the tag, leaving a blank area for the embroidery.

4. Refer to Silk Ribbon Stitches on pages 59-60 to make a simple seven-petal flower using the Japanese ribbon stitch and pink ribbon.

5. Use the gold ribbon to make a French knot center.

6. Add three lazy daisy leaves around the French knot with the green ribbon.

7. Glue the name card to the center of the folded place card.

8. Glue a pink button at each corner of the name card.

# Napkin and Ribbon Rose Napkin

Finished size: 16" square napkin

## MATERIALS

(for one napkin and napkin holder)

Fabric:
- ◇ Fat quarter pink floral
- ◇ Fat quarter blue floral

Wire-edged ribbon:
- ◇ 14" pink ombre, ⅞" wide
- ◇ 10" soft green, ⅝" wide
- ◇ 1 yd. pink, 2½" wide

Pink sewing thread

Wire cutters

## CUTTING INSTRUCTIONS

From the pink floral, cut:
- ◇ One 17" square

From the blue floral, cut:
- ◇ One 17" square

*The reversible napkin highlights two of the floral fabrics, a pink and a blue, and the ribbon rose napkin holder is much easier to make than it looks! Just a little wire pulling and shaping and it's ready to wrap around the napkin.*

1. To make the ribbon rose, tie a knot at one end of the ⅞" pink ombre ribbon, about 1" from the end.

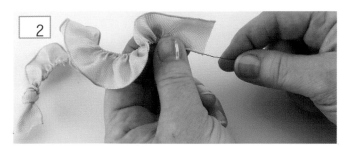

2. To gather the ribbon, pull on one wire. Ombre ribbons generally have a dark edge and a light edge. If you want the dark edge to be the outer petals with a lighter center, pull on the wire on the light side. For the opposite look, pull on the dark side. Pull the wire until it is completely gathered. Do not cut the wire.

3. Holding the knot in one hand, wrap the gathered ribbon around the center, more tightly with the first wraps and then loosely to resemble rose petals. Wrap the wire tightly around the ribbon tail, catching the base of the rose and securing it.

4. To make two leaves, cut the green ribbon in half.

5. Fold each ribbon length in half so the halves of each ribbon are side by side.

## NAPKIN INSTRUCTIONS

Make the napkin with the two fabric squares by following the Reversible Napkin instructions on page 15.

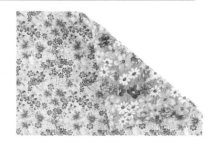

6. Pull the wire from the two inner edges to gather the ribbon.

7. After gathering the center of the leaf, wrap the exposed wires around the raw edges of the ribbon.

8. Sew the leaves to the bottom of the rose. Gather the pink ribbon near the center and sew the rose to the gathered section.

9. Fold the napkin so part of the reverse side shows and wrap the ribbon around the top of the napkin. Tie the ends in a big bow beside the ribbon rose and arrange the tails.

# Apron

Finished size: 11" square bib, 30¼" long skirt

## MATERIALS

Fabric:
- ⅓ yd. floral print for the bib center, backing and bib straps
- ⅛ yd. blue floral for the inner border
- ³⁄₁₆ yd. pink plaid for the outer border and waistband
- 1¼ yd. medium-weight white for the skirt and ties

11½" x 9½" batting

Matching sewing threads

Quilting needle

Quilting thread for hand quilting:
- White

## CUTTING INSTRUCTIONS

From the floral print, cut:
- One 6½" square bib panel
- One 11½" x 9½" backing
- Two 3½" x 22" straps

From the blue floral, cut:
- Two 1" x 6½" inner border strips
- Two 1" x 7½" inner border strips

From the pink plaid, cut:
- Two 2½" x 7½" outer border strips
- One 2½" x 11½" outer border strips
- Two 2¾" x 17½" waistband strips

From the white, cut:
- One 35" x 33" skirt
- Two 4½" x 30 ties

*The bib of the apron is a square version of the place mat. The crisp white fabric of the skirt is gathered and sewn into the plaid waistband for a very pretty and fresh look!*

# INSTRUCTIONS

1. Sew the 6½" blue inner border strips to the sides of the floral print bib panel; press the seams outward.

2. Sew the 7½" blue inner border strips to the top and bottom of the panel; press the seams outward.

3. Sew the 7½" plaid outer border strips to the sides of the panel; press the seams outward.

4. Sew the 11½" outer border strip to the top of the panel; press the seam outward.

5. Fold the pink floral straps in half lengthwise, right sides together. Stitch along the long edge and across one end. Trim the corners; turn the straps right-side out and press.

6. Pin the straps to the top edge of the pieced bib, matching the raw edges of each strap to the raw edge of the top border and having each strap 1¾" in from the corner.

7. Place the batting on your work surface and cover with the floral backing, right-side up. Place the pieced front right-side down on the backing. Pin through all three layers.

8. Stitch around the three bordered sides, leaving the bottom open. Trim the corners. Turn the bib right-side out and press.

9. Machine baste the bottom edges together.

10. Quilt by stitching "in the ditch" between the border and the center panel, and again between the two borders.

11. To hem the skirt, press under ¼" on one 35" edge; press under another 2" and stitch to make the bottom hem.

12. Press ¼" to the wrong side along both 33" sides; press under ¼" again and stitch.

13. Machine stitch two lines of gathering stitches along the remaining long edge of the skirt, ½" and ¼" from the edge.

14. Pull the gathers until the skirt top measures 17" wide.

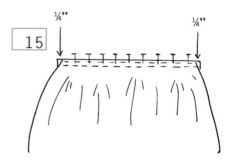

15. Pin the right sides of the gathered skirt to the right side of one plaid waistband piece, leaving ¼" seam allowance on each short end of the waistband. Adjust gathers so they are evenly distributed.

16. Stitch the skirt in place with ½" seam allowance.

17. Center and pin the bottom of the bib front to the remaining long edge of the same waistband piece with the right sides together.

18. Stitch the bib front using ¼" seam allowance.

19. Fold the waist ties in half lengthwise with the right sides together; stitch along the long edge and across one end. Trim the corners, turn right-side out and press.

20. Place the open end of each tie at the end of the waistband with the right sides together, matching the raw edges.

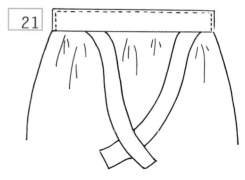

21. Press under ½" on one long edge of the remaining waistband piece. Place this waistband piece right sides together with the stitched waistband, keeping the tie ends between the layers. Stitch along the top and on both ends. Turn right-side out and press.

22. Hand stitch along the bottom long edge to finish the lining.

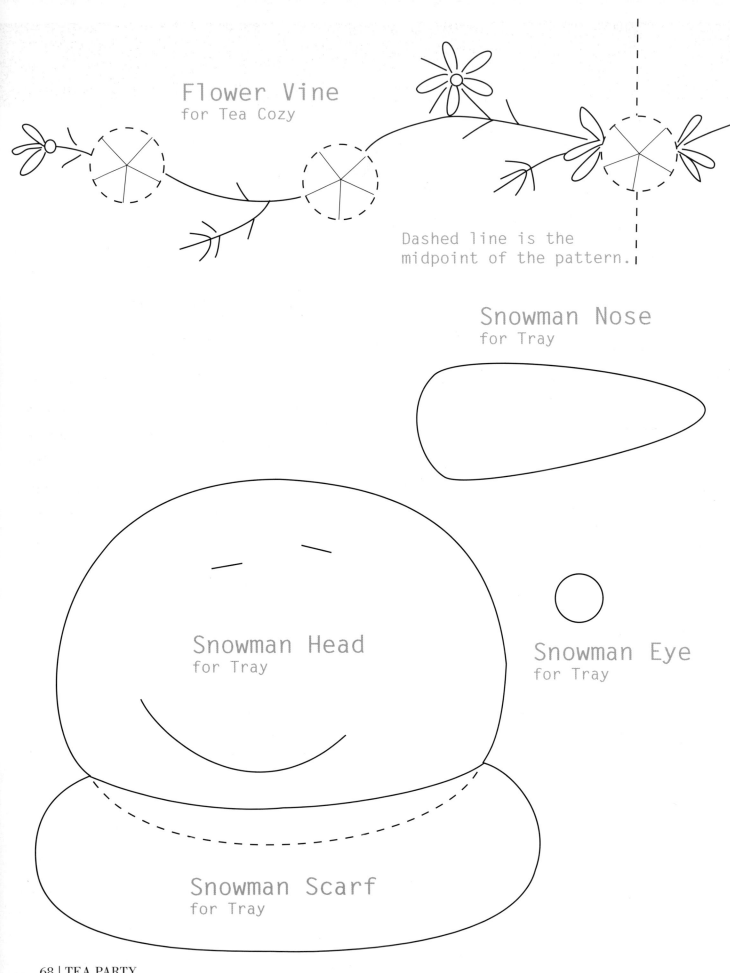

Flower Vine
for Tea Cozy

Dashed line is the
midpoint of the pattern.

Snowman Nose
for Tray

Snowman Head
for Tray

Snowman Eye
for Tray

Snowman Scarf
for Tray

# Snow Buddies

*This coordinating set is perfect for evenings in front of a fire with cookies and hot cocoa. The snowflake polka dots embellish the quilted patchwork table mat, reversible napkins, fabric heart napkin holder, glass cookie jar and wooden tray.*

## FABRIC SELECTION

There are lots of dots here—the polka dots on some of the fabrics are repeated in the painted dots on the tray and cookie jar and even with the many buttons sewn on the quilted table mat. Polka dots give a lighthearted look to this collection, which is fitting for a snowman theme.

# Quilted Table Mat

Finished size: 30" square

## MATERIALS

Fabric:
- ◇ 6-8 assorted fat quarters of blue prints for the patchwork
- ◇ ¼ yd. red print for the inner border
- ◇ 1½ yd. blue print for the outer border and backing
- ◇ Scraps of white, orange and assorted red prints for the appliqués

30½" square batting

Black embroidery floss

12 black buttons for snowman eyes, ¼" diameter

25 assorted white buttons, ½"-¾"

⅛ yd. lightweight fusible interfacing

Matching sewing threads

Embroidery needle

Quilting needle

Quilting thread for hand quilting:
- ◇ Blue
- ◇ Red

Fade-out pen

Freezer paper

Patterns:
- ◇ Snowman Head, page 73
- ◇ Snowman Nose, page 73
- ◇ Snowman Scarf, page 73
- ◇ Heart, page 73

## CUTTING INSTRUCTIONS

From the assorted blue prints, cut:
- ◇ 36 squares (4½")
- ◇ *Note:* It is a good idea to cut a few extra squares; combining the prints involves a lot of switching around to get a good mix.

From the red print, cut:
- ◇ Two 1½" x 24½" inner border strips
- ◇ Two 1½" x 26½" inner border strips

From the blue print fabric, cut:
- ◇ Two 2½" x 26½" outer border strips
- ◇ Two 2½" x 30½" outer border strips
- ◇ One 30½" backing square

*Simple patchwork and appliquéd snowmen and hearts make a jaunty table covering for a kitchen or dining table. The white buttons suggest a sprinkling of snowflakes while they hold the fabric layers together.*

1. Select 12 of the 4½" blue print squares for the appliqué blocks.

2. Draw six snowman heads on the fusible interfacing and cut out. *Note:* Using the fusible interfacing will make the snowman heads appear more opaque on the dark backgrounds.

3. Follow the manufacturer's instructions to fuse the interfacing to the wrong side of the white print fabric with at least ½" between the shapes.

4. Cut out each shape with ¼" margin all around the interfacing.

5. Draw six each of the appliqué patterns—snowman head, snowman nose, scarf and heart—on freezer paper and cut out.

6. Follow either of the Freezer Paper techniques starting on page 13 to prepare the appliqués (I used a variety of red prints for the hearts and scarves).

7. Center one heart on each of the six blue print squares and appliqué in place.

8. Appliqué one snowman head on each of the six blue print squares.

9. Add the nose and scarves to each snowman square.

10. Using two strands of black embroidery floss, sew two ¼" black buttons to each face for eyes.

11. Using two strands of black embroidery floss, make two straight stitches on each face for eyebrows.

12. Draw a curve for a smile on each face with the fade-out pen and backstitch over the line with two strands of black embroidery floss.

13. When all the appliqué squares are complete, begin to lay out the blocks on your work surface as follows: six rows of six blocks each, varying the shades of blue and avoiding having any matching fabrics side by side (refer to the photo). Notice that the snowmen and hearts all face outward along the border in a somewhat random order. When you are satisfied with the arrangement, begin to pin the squares together in each row, being careful to keep the direction of the appliqués correct.

14. Sew the blocks in each row together, pressing the seams in opposing directions for each row.

15. Sew the rows together, matching the seam lines.

16. Sew the 24½" inner border strips to two opposing sides of the pieced top; press the seams outward.

17. Sew the 26½" inner border strips to the remaining sides; press the seams outward.

18. Sew the 26½" outer border strips to two opposing sides of the pieced top; press the seams outward.

19. Sew the 30½" outer border strips to the remaining sides; press the seams outward.

20. Refer to the Self-Binding instructions on page 10 to add the backing and batting.

21. To finish, quilt by stitching "in the ditch" between the red border and the pieced center and between the two borders with matching quilting thread.

22. Sew a white button to each intersection of the patchwork with doubled white thread, sewing through all the layers.

# Napkin and Fabric Heart Napkin Holder

Finished size: 16" square napkin, 3¼" heart on napkin holder

## MATERIALS

(for one napkin and one napkin holder)

Fabric:
- Fat quarter blue print
- ⅔ yd. red print
- Scrap of coordinating red print
- Scrap of fleece

White button, 1⅛" diameter

24" white wire edged ribbon, ⅝" wide

Matching sewing thread

Patterns:
- Heart, page 73

## CUTTING INSTRUCTIONS

From the blue print, cut:
- One 16" square

From the red print, cut:
- One 20" square

From the coordinating red print, cut:
- One 4" x 8" rectangle

From the fleece, cut:
- One 4" square

*The red-and-blue bordered reversible napkin really is fun to fold and tuck into the padded heart napkin holder. The white ribbon and button set off the bright colors.*

# NAPKIN HOLDER INSTRUCTIONS

1. Fold the red rectangle in half, right sides together, and trace the heart pattern on one side.

2. Layer the folded red fabric over the fleece square and make a heart following the instructions for Fleece Padding on page 11.

3. After pressing the completed heart, topstitch ¼" from the edge with matching thread.

4. Sew the white button to the center of the heart front.

5. With the same thread, attach the ribbon to the back of the heart about 11" from one end.

6. Fold the napkin and wrap the longer end of the ribbon around the napkin. Tie the ends in a bow right beside the heart.

# NAPKIN INSTRUCTIONS

1. Follow the instructions in Reversible Napkin with Border on page 15 using the 16" blue square and the 20" red square.

Heart
for Table Mat
and Napkin Holder

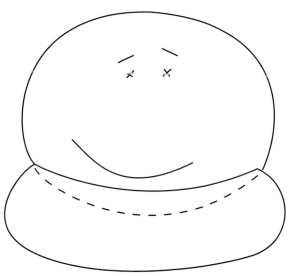

Snowman Head
for Table Mat
and Cookie Jar

Snowman Scarf
for Table Mat
and Cookie Jar

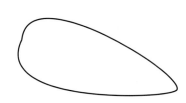

Snowman Nose
for Table Mat
and Cookie Jar

# Snowman Cookie Jar

## MATERIALS

Fabric:
- 2 scraps of blue prints (matching or contrasting)
- Scraps of white, orange and red prints for the appliqués

Glass jar with screw-on lid (model has a 4¼"-diameter lid)

2 black buttons for eyes, ¼" diameter

¾ yd. red jumbo rick rack

1 yd. white ribbon, ¾" wide

Black embroidery floss

Small piece of lightweight fusible interfacing

Matching sewing threads

Rubber band (large enough to fit around the lid of the glass jar)

Surface conditioner and clear gloss glaze for painting glass

White paint for glass

Disposable plate for palette

Bristle or foam brush

Pencil with an unused eraser

Pattern:
- Snowman Head, page 73
- Snowman Scarf, page 73
- Snowman Nose, page 73

## CUTTING INSTRUCTIONS

From the blue prints, cut:
- 2 circles (8¼" diameter)

*The painted snowflake dots combined with the appliquéd snowman lid cover make a lighthearted kitchen accessory.*

1. Draw the snowman head, scarf and nose patterns on the fusible interfacing; cut out. *Note:* Using the fusible interfacing will make the snowman head appear more opaque on the dark backgrounds.

2. Follow the manufacturer's instructions to fuse the interfacing to the wrong side of the white print fabric.

3. Cut out with ¼" margin all around the interfacing.

4. Draw one snowman head, scarf and nose on freezer paper and cut out.

5. Follow either of the Freezer Paper techniques starting on page 13 to prepare the appliqué.

6. Appliqué one snowman head on one blue print circle.

7. Place the rick rack around the outside edge of the appliquéd fabric circle on the right side. Hand baste and then machine stitch the trim in place so the center of the rick rack falls on the ¼" seam line.

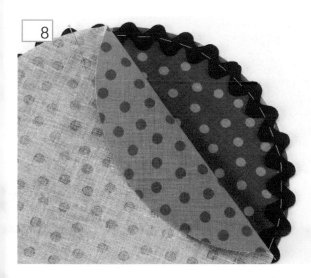

8. Pin the remaining blue circle, right sides together, over the cover front.

9. Sew all around, leaving a 3" opening for turning.

10. Clip the curves and turn the cover right-side out. Fold in the seam allowance on the opening and hand sew the opening closed.

11. To paint the dots of the jar, follow the glass paint manufacturer's instructions to clean and condition the jar.

12. Pour a small puddle of white paint on the palette and dip the eraser end of the pencil in the paint. Touch the eraser to the glass and lift it straight up. Re-dip the eraser and continue around the jar painting random dots. If a dot does not come out very round, re-touch it with the eraser. Let the paint dry and follow the manufacturer's instructions to add a gloss finish to the jar.

13. To add the cover, screw the lid onto the jar. Hold the cover over the lid and slide a rubber band around the cover on the side edge of the lid. Adjust the fabric so the cover is centered and tie a ribbon around the lid to cover the rubber band.

# Fabric Decoupage Tray
Finished size: 15" x 11"

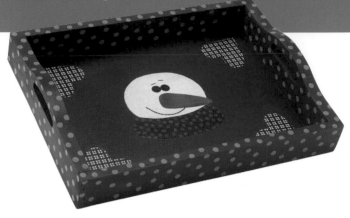

## MATERIALS

Fabric:
- ◇ Small amounts of white, orange and red prints
- ◇ Scrap of black solid

15" x 11" wooden tray

Black embroidery floss

Fusible web

Acrylic paint:
- ◇ Blue
- ◇ White

Decoupage finish

Spray matte finish

Pencil with an unused eraser

Disposable plate for palette

Bristle or foam brush

Sandpaper

Brown paper bag

Pressing cloth

Patterns:
- ◇ Snowman Head, page 68
- ◇ Snowman Nose, page 68
- ◇ Snowman Scarf, page 68
- ◇ Snowman Eye, page 68
- ◇ Heart, page 77

*Paint, dot and decorate a wooden tray. Fabric cutouts with a decoupage finish make this project as functional as it is attractive.*

1. If needed, sand the wood tray and wipe it clean.

2. Apply a coat of blue acrylic paint to the tray and let it dry.

3. Lightly sand the painted coat with the brown paper, which is good for smoothing the grain that raises with the wet paint.

4. Apply a second coat and smooth the surface again.

5. For the dots, mix a little white paint into the blue for a lighter shade.

6. Dip the pencil eraser into the paint and touch it to the side of the tray, forming a dot. Re-dip the eraser for each dot. Dot the sides of the tray, inside and out, but leave the inside plain.

7. Draw the snowman head, nose, scarf, two eyes and four hearts on the paper side of the fusible web. Refer to Fusible Appliqué on page 12 to prepare the fabric pieces.

8. Before fusing the pieces on the tray, lightly draw a curved smile on the snowman with a pencil. Backstitch on the line using two strands of black floss.

9. Determine where the eyes will be and make two straight stitches for eyebrows.

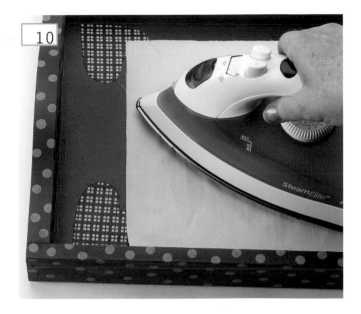

10. Place the snowman pieces on the center of the tray. When satisfied with the arrangement, cover the appliqué with a pressing cloth and fuse in place.

11. Repeat, fusing a heart in each corner.

12. Use the brush to spread the decoupage finish over the inside of the tray. Let dry.

13. Apply a second coat of decoupage finish. Let dry.

14. When the tray is completely dry, spray it with a matte finish.

Heart
for Tray

# Coffee Klatch

*You can almost smell the roasting coffee beans when you work on this set of coffee-related projects. An informal get-together with friends—a klatch— is the inspiration for this collection, which includes an appliquéd and quilted table mat, napkins and napkin holders, a set of fun coasters and a lined bread basket embellished with an expressive mini quilt.*

## FABRIC SELECTION

Color, pattern and texture all have a role in this collection. For a coffee theme, a variety of warm brown and creamy tan prints seem most appropriate. Fabrics with coffee cup motifs and swirls resembling steam really set the mood while the touch of red brightens up the look. Textured additions, such as the osnaburg fabric and the jute cord, bring to mind big sacks of coffee beans.

# Quilted Table Mat
Finished size: 28" square

## MATERIALS

Fabric:
- ⅛ yd. each of 9 different brown and tan fabrics for the nine-patch blocks
- ¼ yd. tan print for the appliquéd blocks
- ¼ yd. red-and-brown check for the border and appliqués
- 1¼ yd. brown-and-red print for the outer border and backing
- Scrap of red solid for the appliqués

28½" square batting

Dark brown embroidery floss

Matching sewing thread

Quilting thread for hand quilting:
- Red
- Brown
- Ecru

Fusible web

Quilting needle

Embroidery needle

Fade-out pen

Patterns:
- Coffee Cup, page 81
- Handle, page 81
- Saucer, page 81
- Inner Cup, page 81

## CUTTING INSTRUCTIONS

From the brown and tan, cut:
- Five 3" squares *from each fabric*

From the tan print, cut:
- Four 8" squares

From the red-and-brown check, cut:
- Two 1¼" x 23" inner border strips
- Two 1¼" x 24½" inner border strips

From the brown-and-red print, cut:
- Two 2½" x 24½" outer border strips
- Two 2½" x 28½" outer border strips
- One 28½" square backing

*Nine-patch blocks using coffee-colored fabrics and steaming coffee cup appliqués will make you thirsty for friends to chat with.*

1. For each nine-patch block, lay nine brown and tan 3" squares out in a pattern of three rows of three squares each (each block is identical).

2. Sew the squares of each row together, pressing the seams in opposing directions for each row.

3. Sew the rows together, matching the seam lines. Repeat for a total of five 8" square blocks.

4. Trace four each of the coffee cup, handle, saucer and inner cup on the paper side of the fusible web and refer to Fusible Appliqués on page 12 to prepare the pieces, using the red solid fabric for the inner cup and the red-and-brown check for the remaining pieces.

5. Arrange the cup and saucer appliqués on the tan print square with the bottom of the saucer about 1¾" up from the bottom edge of the block. Fuse in place.

6. Finish the edges of the appliqué with a blanket stitch using two strands of dark brown floss.

7. Transfer the steam lines for the coffee cup with the fade-out pen and stem stitch over the lines with one strand of floss.

8. Arrange the prepared blocks into three rows of three blocks each, with the bottom of the cup and saucer always near the outer edge. Sew the rows together, matching the seam lines.

9. Sew the 23" red-and-brown check inner border strips to two opposing sides of the pieced top; press the seams outward.

10. Sew the 24½" red-and-brown check inner border strips to the remaining sides; press the seams outward.

11. Sew the 24½" brown-and-red print outer border strips to two opposing sides of the bordered top; press the seams outward.

12. Sew the 28½" brown-and-red print outer border strips to the remaining sides; press the seams outward.

13. Layer the backing, batting and pieced top and follow the Self-Binding instructions on page 10.

14. Quilt "in the ditch" between each block, then between the blocks and the red border, and also between the two borders using matching quilting thread.

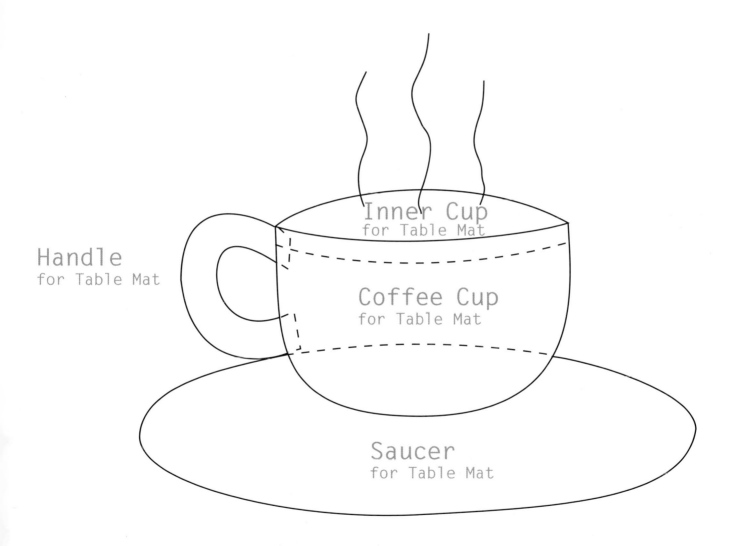

Handle
for Table Mat

Inner Cup
for Table Mat

Coffee Cup
for Table Mat

Saucer
for Table Mat

# Napkin and Napkin Holder

Finished size: 17" square napkin

## MATERIALS

(for one napkin and one napkin holder):

Fabric:
- ◇ Fat quarter coffee print

Brown button, 1⅛" diameter

Red heart button, ⅝" across

24" jute

Matching sewing thread

Dark brown embroidery floss

Permanent fabric adhesive

## CUTTING INSTRUCTIONS

From the coffee print, cut:
- ◇ One 18" square

*Ordinary hemmed napkins become special accessories when made with a coffee cup print. The napkin is folded and wrapped with a super-simple button and jute holder.*

# NAPKIN HOLDER INSTRUCTIONS

1. Place the red heart button over the brown button, matching the holes and sew together with dark brown floss. Do not cut the floss. *Note:* You may wish to glue the buttons together first, but avoid gluing close to the holes.

2. Using the same floss, sew the buttons to the jute about 9" from one end. Tie a knot at each end of the jute.

3. Fold the napkin in half and then in thirds. Wrap the long end of the jute around the back of the napkin and tie the ends in a bow beside the buttons.

## NAPKIN INSTRUCTIONS

1. Press ¼" hem all around the 18" coffee print square.

2. Fold the hem again so it is doubled and press well.

3. Use a few pins to hold the hem in place and stitch all around.

# Coffee Mug Coasters

Finished size: 4" square

## MATERIALS

(for a set of four coasters)

Fabric:
- ◇ Fat quarter tea-bag osnaburg for the center
- ◇ ⅛ yd. brown mini check for the borders and backing
- ◇ Scrap of fleece

Dark brown embroidery floss

Matching sewing thread

Pencil

Embroidery hoop

Embroidery needle

Patterns:
- ◇ Cup o' Joe, page 85
- ◇ House Blend, page 85
- ◇ Java, page 85
- ◇ Latte, page 85

## CUTTING INSTRUCTIONS

From the tea-bag osnaburg, cut:
- ◇ One 10" center square

From the fleece, cut:
- ◇ Four 4½" squares

From the brown mini check, cut:
- ◇ Four 4½" squares
- ◇ Eight 1¼" x 3" border strips
- ◇ Eight 1¼" x 4½" border strips

*These coasters are just the thing for a coffee aficionado. Stitch the coffee-related words on a dark osnaburg fabric and trim with a brown mini check.*

1. Draw a 6" square in the center of the osnaburg center with a pencil; divide that into four 3" squares and mark with the pencil.

2. Transfer one coffee word to the center of each 3" square with the fade-out pen.

3. Place the fabric in an embroidery hoop and backstitch over the lines with two strands of dark brown floss. Make a French knot for each dot.

4. Cut out each square on the penciled line.

5. Sew the 3" border strips to two opposing sides of each stitched center; press the seams outward.

6. Sew the 4½" border strips to the two remaining sides of each stitched center; press the seams outward.

7. To assemble each coaster, layer the fleece, backing and embroidered front and follow the Self-Binding instructions on page 10.

8. To finish the coasters, sew a running stitch all around the center square, close to the border with two strands of embroidery floss.

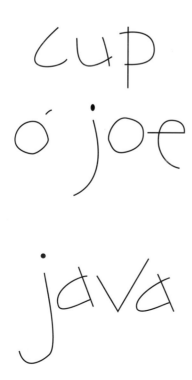

cup
o' joe

latte

java

house
blend

# Lined Basket with Mini Quilt
Finished size: 8" x 4" mini quilt

## MATERIALS

Fabric:
- ¼ yd. natural osnaburg
- ⅛ yd. brown print for the backing and one border of the mini quilt
- Scraps of three coordinating brown prints for the borders
- ½ yd. red-and-brown check for the basket lining

Basket (Model is 8¾" x 5")

Batting

2 yd. brown grosgrain ribbon, ¾" wide

Dark brown embroidery floss

Lightweight cardboard to fit the bottom of the basket

Embroidery hoop

Embroidery needle

Fade-out pen

Permanent fabric adhesive

Patterns:
- Quote, page 88

## CUTTING INSTRUCTIONS

From the brown print, cut:
- One 1¼" x 7" border strip
- One 8½" x 4½" backing

From the coordinating brown prints, cut:
- One 1¼" x 7" border strip
- Two 1¼" x 4½" border strips

From the batting, cut:
- One 8½" x 4½" rectangle

*The sentiment is so true—and the basket makes a perfect holder for breads or biscotti. This would make a wonderful gift basket for a good friend!*

# MINI QUILT INSTRUCTIONS

1. Transfer the quote to the center of the osnaburg using the fade-out pen.

2. Place the fabric in an embroidery hoop and backstitch over the lines with two strands of dark brown embroidery floss. Make French knots for the dots.

3. Trim the osnaburg to a 7" x 3" rectangle, centering the quote.

4. Sew the 7" border strips to the top and bottom of the embroidered block; press the seams outward.

5. Sew the 4½" border strips to the sides of the embroidered block; press the seams outward.

6. Layer the backing, batting and embroidered front, following the Self-Binding instructions on page 10.

7. To finish the mini quilt, sew a running stitch all around the center rectangle, close to the border, with two strands of floss.

# BASKET LINING INSTRUCTIONS

1. Measure the height of the side of the basket; measure the perimeter of the opening.

2. To determine the lining strip dimensions, you will need a piece of red-and-brown check that is equal to the basket's height plus 2½" for the width, and 2½ times the perimeter for the length. In equation form:
Lining strip = (basket height + 2½") x (perimenter x 2½)
*Note:* My strip dimensions are 7½" x 68" (two 7½" x 34½" strips were sewn together to reach that measurement).

3. To determine the dimensions of the bottom of the basket, draw a pattern on the cardboard for your basket bottom and cut it out, trimming the edges until it slips easily into place in the basket. Cut a piece of fabric 1" larger all around than the cardboard and a piece of batting to fit the cardboard.

4. Glue the batting to one side of the cardboard.

5. Hand-sew gathering stitches around the edge of the fabric for the bottom.

6. Place the cardboard, batting side down, on the wrong side of the fabric. Pull the stitches so the fabric pulls snugly over the edge of the cardboard. Set this piece aside.

7. Sew the short ends of the lining strips together to form a tube.

8. Press under a 1¾" hem along one long edge of the tube for the top. Machine sew two lines of gathering stitches 1⅛" and 1" from the fold.

9. Machine sew one line of gathering stitches ½" from the bottom edge of the tube.

10. Pull the bobbin threads on the top gathers from both ends until the tube is approximately the size of the basket's inner diameter. Repeat with the bottom gathers. Knot the threads on one end only, leaving the other end free to make adjustments.

11. Place the gathered tube inside the basket and begin to adjust the gathers until the lining fits and the gathers are evenly distributed. *Note:* It is better to leave it slightly loose than to have it too tight because you can ease extra fabric in with the gluing step.

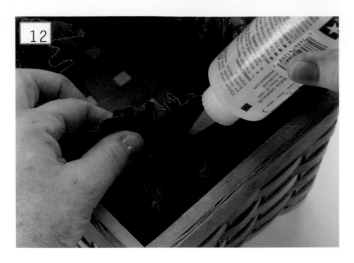

**12.** Apply glue to the gathered lines on the wrong side of the liner, just a few inches at a time, and press it to the inside top edge of the basket. *Note:* The edge of the lining should extend about ¾" at the top and the other gathering stitches should touch the bottom of the basket. Glue the lining in place all around the top edge.

**13.** Apply glue to the bottom of the basket along the edge and pull the lining straight down, pressing the edge into the glue. Work just a small section at a time.

**14.** Apply glue to the bottom of the basket and slip the padded bottom inside. Press it down to adhere it to the basket.

**15.** Starting in the back of the basket near one corner, glue a length of ribbon around the inside of the basket, covering the gathering stitches. Overlap the ends and trim off the excess ribbon.

**16.** To cover the ribbon ends, cut a 5" length of ribbon and tie a knot in the center. Glue the knot over the ribbon ends and make a V-cut on the ends of the loose ribbon.

**17.** Tie the remaining ribbon around the outside of the basket just under the rim. Tie the ends in a knot at one front corner and trim the ends in a V-cut.

**18.** Center the mini quilt on the front side of the basket. Glue the top back of the quilt to the ribbon.

Quote
for Mini Quilt

The Perfect Blend...
Good Coffee,
Good Friends

## MATERIALS

Fabric:
- ◇ Scrap of natural osnaburg to fit in an embroidery hoop
- ◇ Scrap of brown mini check

Wood memo holder with pad (6¾" x 6")

Scrap of extra-loft batting (to fit the small dome pattern)

Dark brown embroidery floss

18" brown grosgrain ribbon, ⅜" wide

2 brown buttons, ¾" diameter

Fusible web

Small piece of lightweight cardboard

Acrylic paint:
- ◇ Cream

Spray matte finish

Spray caramel-color suede finish

Sandpaper

Paintbrush

Embroidery hoop

Embroidery needle

Fade-out pen

Permanent fabric adhesive

Patterns:
- ◇ Espresso Yourself, page 91
- ◇ Small Dome, page 91
- ◇ Large Dome, page 91

## CUTTING INSTRUCTIONS

From the natural osnaburg, cut:
- ◇ One 2⅝" x 4" rectangle
- ◇ One 8" square

*Espresso yourself on this handy memo pad. The expression is hand stitched and attached to a purchased wood notepad holder. The cover of the pad is painted and decorated to coordinate with the set.*

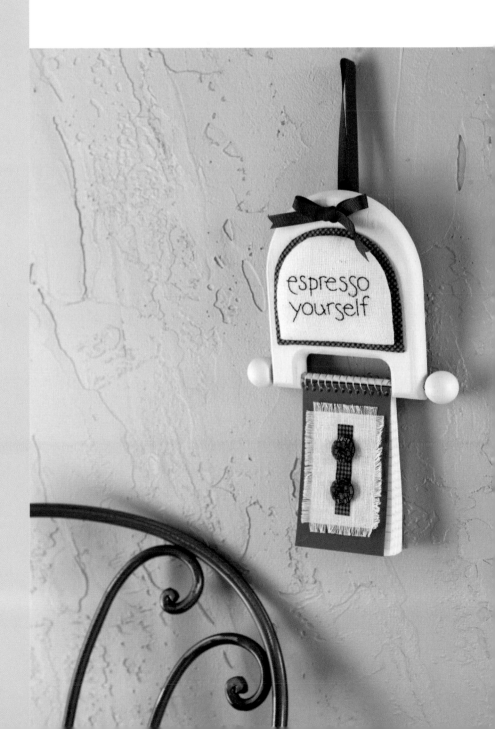

**1.** Sand the memo holder with sandpaper if necessary and wipe clean.

**2.** Paint the holder with the cream paint; let dry.

**3.** Sand the holder lightly.

**4.** Apply a second coat of paint. Let dry.

**5.** When the second coat is dry, spray with matte finish.

**6.** Transfer the saying to the center of the osnaburg square using the fade-out pen.

**7.** Place the fabric in the embroidery hoop and backstitch over the lines using the dark brown embroidery floss.

**8.** Cut one of each of the small dome and large dome shapes from the cardboard.

**9.** Cut the stitched osnaburg 1" larger on all sides than the smaller dome.

**10.** Cut the brown check 1" larger than the bigger dome. Save the scraps to decorate the cover of the pad.

**11.** Glue a piece of batting to the small cardboard dome; trim the edges to fit the cardboard.

**12.** Place the osnaburg fabric, stitched-side down, on the table; place the cardboard on the fabric, batting side down. Glue the edges of the fabric to the back of the cardboard, checking the front to be sure that the lettering is straight across and centered.

**13.** Cover the larger cardboard dome with the brown check fabric in the same way (without batting).

**14.** Glue the back of the stitched piece to the front of the fabric piece. Glue them to the front of the message board.

**15.** To change the color of the notepad, twist the wire spirals at the top to release the pad. Keep the pages intact and remove the covers. Cover them with a spray-on suede finish on the inside and outside, following the directions on the can. When the finish is dry, put the papers back between the covers, lining up the holes, and insert the end of the spiral wire back into the first hole on one end. Twist the wire to re-attach it to the pad.

## TIP

When the pad gets full, remove the covers and attach them to a new pad.

**16.** Fringe the edges of the 2⅝" x 4" osnaburg rectangle.

**17.** Draw a ½" x 2¾" rectangle on the paper side of the fusible web. Follow the manufacturer's instructions to apply it to the wrong side of a scrap of brown mini check fabric.

**18.** Cut out the brown mini check on the lines and fuse this to the center of the osnaburg.

**19.** Glue the osnaburg to the center of the pad cover.

**20.** Glue the two buttons on the fabric strip.

**21.** Hang the pad on the dowel in the memo holder.

**22.** Fold the ribbon in half and tie a knot 4" down from the top of the loop. Push the loop through the hole in the memo holder, from the front to the back. Tie a bow on the front with the ribbon ends.

Small Dome
for Message Board

espresso
yourself

Large Dome
for Message Board

# Family Fare

Family meal time should be an occasion for family togetherness—talking, sharing and enjoying favorite foods. The bright colors and simple shapes of the patchwork house create an informal and lively mood.

## FABRIC SELECTION

For this set of projects with a theme of family, I chose homespuns in a variety of bright colors and patterns. It's animated and cheerful, just right for a family gathering. The texture of the homespuns, the plaid and check patterns, and the fun colors all contribute to a warm and casual mood.

# Place Mat and Napkin

Finished size: 17½" x 12½" place mat, 18" square napkin

## MATERIALS

(for one place mat and napkin)

Fabric:
- ◇ ³⁄₁₆ yd. natural color solid for the place mat panel and backing
- ◇ ½ yd. yellow homespun for the background, window and napkin
- ◇ ⅛ yd. blue plaid homespun for the house and binding
- ◇ Scrap of red plaid homespun for the heart, door and roof
- ◇ Scraps of 6 assorted green plaid and check homespuns for the ground
- ◇ Scrap of fleece

17½" x 12½" batting

Red button, ½" diameter

Matching sewing threads

Quilting thread for hand quilting:
- ◇ Green
- ◇ Yellow
- ◇ Blue

Quilting needle

Freezer paper

Masking tape or quilter's tape

Patterns:
- ◇ Door, page 95
- ◇ Window, page 95
- ◇ Heart, page 95

## CUTTING INSTRUCTIONS

From the natural solid, cut:
- ◇ One 11½" x 12½" panel
- ◇ One 17½" x 12½" backing

From the blue plaid homespun, cut:
- ◇ One 5" x 4" house
- ◇ 2" wide binding strips (so they measure 2" x 65" when seamed)

From the yellow homespun, cut:
- ◇ Two 1¼" x 4" background strips
- ◇ Two 3" background squares
- ◇ One 6½" x 2½" background strips
- ◇ One 18" square

From the red plaid homespun, cut:
- ◇ One 6½" x 3" roof
- ◇ Two 5" x 4" rectangles

From the assorted green plaid and check homespuns, cut:
- ◇ Six 2½" squares (one from each fabric)

From the fleece, cut:
- ◇ One 4" x 5" rectangle

Pieces for the house panel.

*Make a family house of patchwork squares and rectangles with an appliqué door and window. Hold the fringed napkin in place with a fabric heart. With so many colors in this set, each family member could have a different colored napkin.*

1. Use the patterns to draw a door and window onto freezer paper. Refer to Freezer Paper Appliqués on page 13 to prepare the appliqués. *Note:* The bottom of the door is *not* turned under, as it will be in the seam.

2. Pin the door to the house with the bottom raw edges matching and the side of the door about ¾" from the right side of the house. Pin the window to the left side of the house. Hand stitch the appliqués in place.

3. Lay the six green squares out in two rows of three squares each. Sew each row together.

4. Sew the two rows of green together to make one block 6½" x 4½".

5. Sew the yellow strips to the sides of the house, making a block 6½" x 4".

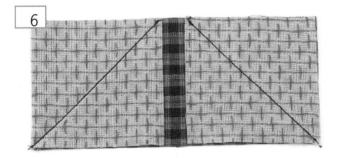

6. Sew the yellow squares to the roof rectangle by first marking a diagonal line on the wrong side of each yellow square from corner to corner. Pin a yellow square to each end of the red roof, right sides together with the diagonal going up, and stitch on these marked seam lines.

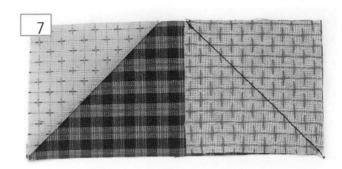

7. Trim the seam allowance of the diagonal seams to ¼" and flip the yellow sections up and over so they form the upper corners of the 6½" x 3" block. Press the seams toward the roof.

8. Sew the 6½" yellow strip to the top of the roof; press the seams upward.

9. Sew the bottom of the roof to the top of the house; press the seams upward.

10. Sew the bottom of the house to the top of the ground; press the seams upward.

11. Sew the long edge of the 11½" x 12½" natural solid panel to the left side of the house panel; press the seam away from the house.

12. Assemble the layers following the Backing, Batting and Basting instructions on page 9.

13. Quilt the house block as follows:
    ◊ Use green thread to quilt diagonal lines through the ground block and between the house and ground (lay a piece of low tack masking tape or quilters tape down as a guide for the diagonal lines)
    ◊ Use yellow thread to quilt around the house and between the yellow strip and the roof top
    ◊ Use yellow to quilt the window panes by stitching through the center of the window vertically and horizontally
    ◊ Use blue to quilt around the door and between the roof and house

14. Sew the red button to the door for a doorknob, sewing through all the layers.

15. Prepare the binding and sew it to the place mat following the Applied Binding instructions on page 10.

**16.** For the heart napkin holder, trace the heart pattern onto the wrong side of one 5" x 4" red plaid rectangle. Refer to Fleece Padding on page 11 to complete the heart. Top-stitch ¼" from the edge with matching thread.

**17.** To attach the heart, place the heart close to the edge of the place mat about 4" down from the top. Use small appliqué stitches to sew the outer side edge of the heart to the mat. Cup the heart so there is room to hold a napkin and sew the other side in place.

Refer to Fleece Padding on page 11

## NAPKIN INSTRUCTIONS

**1.** Follow the Fringed Edge instructions on page 15 using the 18" yellow square.

**2.** Fold the napkin and slide it under the heart on the place mat.

Follow the Fringed Edge instructions on page 15

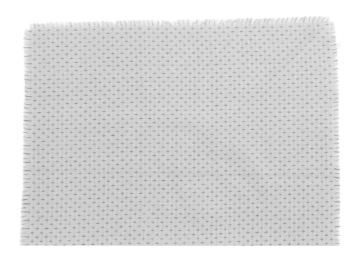

Door
for Place Mat,
Hot Pad and
Recipe Album

Window
for Place Mat,
Hot Pad and
Recipe Album

Heart
for Place Mat

# Hot Pad

Finished size: 9" square

## MATERIALS

Fabric:
- ◇ Scrap of yellow plaid homespun for the background and window
- ◇ Scrap of blue plaid homespun for the house
- ◇ Scrap of red plaid homespun for the roof and door
- ◇ Scrap of green homespun for the backing
- ◇ Scraps of 4 assorted green plaid and check homespuns for the border

⅜ yd. batting

Red button, ½" diameter

Matching sewing threads

Yellow quilting thread

Freezer paper

Patterns:
- ◇ Door, page 95
- ◇ Window, page 95

## CUTTING INSTRUCTIONS

From the blue plaid homespun, cut:
- ◇ One 5" x 4" house

From the yellow plaid homespun, cut:
- ◇ Two 1¼" x 4" strips
- ◇ Two 3" squares

From the red plaid homespun, cut:
- ◇ One 6½" x 3" roof

From the green homespun, cut:
- ◇ One 9½" square backing

From the assorted green plaid and check homespuns, cut:
- ◇ Two 2" x 6½" border strips
- ◇ Two 2" x 9½" border strips
- ◇ *Note:* Use a different green fabric for each strip.

From the batting, cut:
- ◇ Two 9½" squares

*The house motif from the place mat continues in this project with a green fabric border. The thick layer of batting makes this pad a practical accessory for the kitchen.*

# INSTRUCTIONS

1. Use the patterns to draw a door and window onto freezer paper. Prepare the appliqués following the Freezer Paper Appliqué instructions on page 13. *Note:* The bottom of the door is *not* turned under, as it will be in the seam.

2. Pin the door to the house with the bottom raw edges matching and the side of the door about ¾" from the right side of the house. Pin the window to the left side of the house. Hand stitch the appliqués in place.

3. Sew through the center of the window vertically and horizontally to make panes with yellow quilting thread.

4. Sew the yellow strips to the sides of the house.

5. Sew the yellow squares to the roof rectangle by first marking a diagonal line on the wrong side of each yellow square from corner to corner. Pin a yellow square to each end of the red roof, right sides together with the diagonal going up, and stitch on these marked seam lines.

6. Trim the seam allowance of the diagonal seams to ¼" and flip the yellow sections up and over so they form the upper corners of the 6½" x 3" block. Press the seams toward the roof.

7. Sew the roof block and the house block together.

8. Sew the 6½" green border strips to the top and bottom of the house block; press the seams outward.

9. Sew the 9½" green border strips to each side; press the seams outward.

10. Layer the two batting pieces, backing and pieced top and follow the instructions in Self-Binding on page 10 to assemble the hot pad.

11. Since the hot pad is so thick it is difficult to hand quilt, machine stitch between the house block and the borders.

12. Sew the red button to the door for a doorknob, sewing through all the layers.

## MATERIALS

Fabric:
- ◇ Fat quarter red plaid homespun
- ◇ Fat quarter green plaid homespun
- ◇ Scrap of yellow homespun for the ties

Extra-loft batting

Matching sewing threads

## CUTTING INSTRUCTIONS

From the yellow homespun, cut:
- ◇ Eight 1¼" x 9" strips

*This simple design folds up around the sides of the baking dish when the corners are tied. Using two contrasting fabrics makes it reversible, to coordinate with every occasion.*

1. To make a cover to fit your baking dish, place the dish on a piece of fabric and hold up the sides of the fabric to fit. Add 1" to your measurements for ease and seam allowance. *Note:* If your dish is square and has an extra lip for a handle on two sides, cut it square, but use the wider measurement. If it is rectangular, you will have two measurements.

2. Cut one red, one green and one batting piece to this measurement.

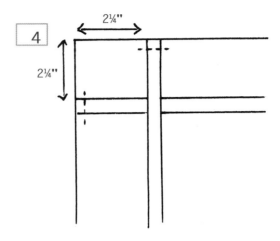

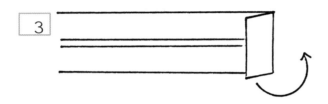

3. To make the ties, fold both long sides into the center of one yellow strip and press. Then press under ½" hem on the short end of the strip. Fold and press the strip in half lengthwise and sew close to the edge. Repeat with the remaining strips to make a total of eight ties.

4. Pin one end of each tie 2¼" in from a corner on one of the fabric squares, matching the raw edges. Baste in place.

5. Hold the two fabric squares right sides together, and place them on the batting square; pin all three layers together. Sew all around, leaving a 4" opening on one side for turning. Clip the corners and trim the batting close to the seam. Turn the cover right sides out and press.

6. Fold the seam allowance in on the opening and hand sew the edges of the opening closed.

7. To use the cover, set the baking dish in the center and pull the sides of the cover up by tying the yellow cords in a bow at each corner.

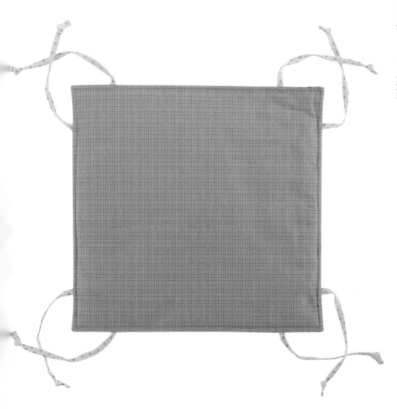

# Quilted Recipe Album

Finished size: 8⅜" x 13⅜" closed

## MATERIALS

Fabric:
- ½ yd. natural-color solid for the album cover
- Scrap of yellow plaid homespun for the background and window
- Scrap of blue plaid homespun for the house
- Scrap of red plaid homespun for the roof, heart and door
- Scraps of 6 assorted green plaid and check homespuns for the ground

3-ring photo album with slip-in pockets for 6" x 4" photos (8⅜" x 13⅜")

Batting

4 cream-color buttons, ⅞" diameter

4 cream-color buttons, ⅝" diameter

Black embroidery floss

6" x 4" index or recipe cards

Lightweight cardboard

Matching sewing threads

Quilting thread:
- Green
- Yellow
- Blue

Quilting needle

Embroidery hoop

Masking or quilter's tape

Fusible web

Black fine tip permanent marker

Freezer paper

Pinking shears

Fray preventative

Permanent fabric adhesive

Patterns:
- Door, page 95
- Window, page 95
- Family Fare, page 103
- Small Heart, page 103

## CUTTING INSTRUCTIONS

From the natural-color solid, cut:
- Two 6½" x 3⅞" strips (A)
- One 3⅜" x 17⅜" strip (B)
- One 13¾" x 17⅜" rectangle (C)
- Two 2" x 12⅜" strips

From the blue plaid homespun, cut:
- One 5" x 4" house

From the yellow plaid homespun, cut:
- Two 1¼" x 4" strips
- Two 3" squares

From the red plaid homespun, cut:
- One 6½" x 3" roof

From the assorted green plaid and check homespuns, cut:
- Six 2½" squares (one from each fabric)
- Two 6½" x 4½" rectangles (from one fabric only)

Every family has a collection of favorite recipes, sometimes scribbled on scraps of paper and jammed in a drawer with other clippings. How handy to have them all in one place in an album that you can display. This album repeats the quilted house motif on its cover and has an inside pocket for extra recipe cards.

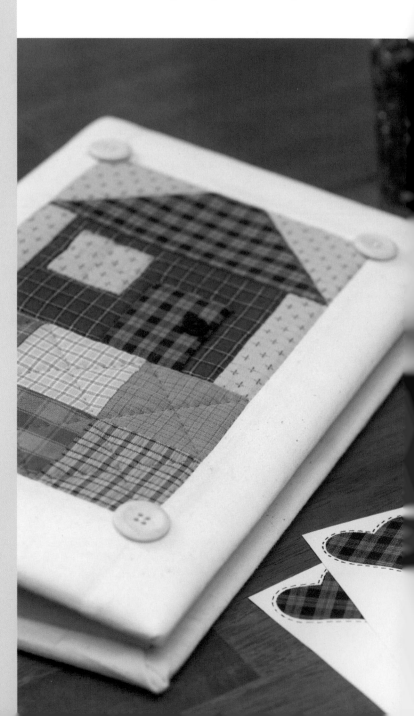

1. Use the patterns to draw a door and window onto freezer paper. Refer to Freezer Paper Appliqués on page 13 to prepare the appliqués. The bottom of the door is *not* turned under, as it will be in the seam.

2. Pin the door to the house with the bottom raw edges matching and the side of the door about ¾" from the right side of the house. Pin the window to the left side of the house. Hand stitch the appliqués in place.

3. Lay the six green squares out in two rows of three squares each. Sew each row together.

4. Sew the two rows of green together to make one block 6½" x 4½".

5. Sew the yellow strips to the sides of the house, making a block 6½" x 4".

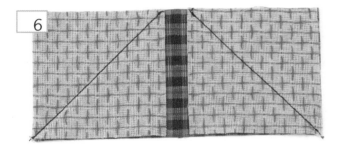

6. Sew the yellow squares to the roof rectangle by first marking a diagonal line on the wrong side of each yellow square from corner to corner. Pin a yellow square to each end of the red roof, right sides together with the diagonal going up, and stitch on these marked seam lines.

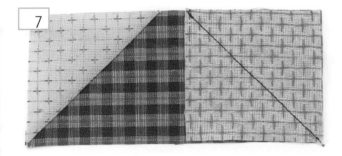

7. Trim the seam allowance of the diagonal seams to ¼" and flip the yellow sections up and over so they form the upper corners of the 6½" x 3" block. Press the seams toward the roof.

8. Sew the bottom of the roof to the top of the house; press the seams upward.

9. Sew the bottom of the house to the top of the ground; press the seams upward.

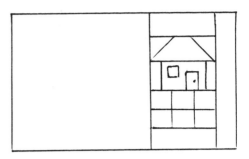

10. To assemble the album cover, sew the two A strips to the top and bottom of the house block; press the seams outward.

11. Sew the B strip to the right of the house; press the seams outward.

12. Sew the C piece to the left of the house; press the seams outward.

13. Cut a piece of batting to fit the album when it is open.

14. Center the batting on the back of the pieced fabric and baste together.

15. Quilt the house block as follows:
◇ Use green thread to quilt diagonal lines through the ground block and between the house and ground (lay a piece of low tack masking tape or quilters tape down as a guide for the diagonal lines).
◇ Use yellow thread to quilt around the house and between the yellow strip and the roof top.
◇ Use yellow thread to quilt the window panes by stitching through the center of the window vertically and horizontally.
◇ Use blue thread to quilt around the door and between the roof and house.

16. Sew the red button to the door for the doorknob and the large cream buttons to each corner of the house panel.

17. Press under ¼" along one long side of the 12⅜" natural-color strips. Center and glue one strip along each side of the binder hardware with the folded side against the metal.

18. Place the pieced fabric cover right-side down on the table and center the open album on the fabric. Be sure that the edges of the batting match the edges of the album.

19. Fold the corners of the fabric diagonally over the corners of the album and glue in place.

**20.** Fold the short edges over the side edges of the album and glue in place.

**21.** Fold the long edges of the fabric over the top and bottom edges of the album, trimming the fabric to fit around the binder hardware.

**22.** Apply fray preventative to the trimmed edges; let dry.

**23.** Glue the long edges in place, mitering the corner.

**24.** To cover the inside of the album, cut two pieces of cardboard ½" smaller on all sides than the front and back of the album. *Note:* The front and back measurements may be different depending on where the binder hardware is located.

**25.** Cut two fabric pieces 1" larger on all sides than the cardboard pieces. Set aside.

**26.** To make the inside pocket, place the 6½" x 4½" green rectangles right sides together. Sew all around, leaving a small opening for turning. Trim the corners and turn it right-side out; press.

**27.** Fold in the seam allowance on the opening and hand stitch the folded edges closed.

**28.** Place the rectangle on the right side of the fabric piece cut for the inside front cover, about 4" up from the bottom. Sew around the sides and bottom ¼" from the edge to form a pocket.

**29.** Transfer the words "Family Fare" to a scrap of the cover fabric large enough to fit in the embroidery hoop.

**30.** With the fabric in the hoop, backstitch over the lines.

**31.** Use the heart pattern, red plaid homespun and fusible web to add a red heart appliqué beside the words, referring to Fusible Appliqué on page 12.

**32.** Sew a running stitch around the heart with one strand of floss.

**33.** Trim the pocket to 5" x 3".

**34.** Machine stitch all around, ¼" from the edge. Use the pinking shears to trim the edges.

**35.** Lightly dab glue on the back of the fabric and glue it to the center of the pocket.

**36.** Sew a small cream button to each corner of the pocket.

**37.** Center the cardboard for the front inside cover on the wrong side of the fabric with the pocket. Fold the edges of the fabric over the edges of the cardboard and glue in place. Repeat to cover the back cardboard piece with the plain fabric. Center and glue the covered cardboard pieces inside the front and back of the album.

**38.** To make the recipe cards, fuse red hearts to the upper left corner of the index cards. Draw stitch lines around the heart with a black marker.

Small Heart
for Recipe Album

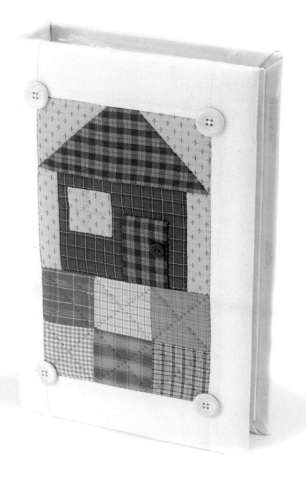

family
fare

# Let's Celebrate!

We have so many occasions for celebration—holidays, birthdays, graduations, promotions, good report cards, first home run—and what better place to come together than the dinner table. The pattern for this set is versitile. The table runner and wine bag in black-and-white are formal, yet the place mat in hot pink, lime green and yellow set a much livlier mood. Both sets include reversible napkins and flowers for corsages or boutonnières.

## FABRIC SELECTION

This chapter shows the difference that color selection can make! The fabrics in both the table runner and the place mat are smooth cottons with a very geometric pattern. Using only black-and-white with a touch of red gives the table runner a more sophisticated look. But substitute vivid colors and the look is much more informal, sunny and fun. Bright primary colors would be fitting for a child's celebration. Holiday colors, such as red and green for Christmas, would carry out the spirit of the season.

# Quilted Table Runner

Finished size: 14½" x 56½"

## MATERIALS

Fabric:
◇ 1 fat quarter each of four geometric black with white prints for blocks
◇ 1 fat quarter each of four geometric white with black prints
◇ 1⅝ yd. black-and-white print for the backing
◇ ³⁄₁₆ yd. red for the binding

16½" x 58½" batting

4 flat red buttons, 1¼" diameter

Matching sewing threads

Quilting thread for hand quilting:
◇ Black

Quilting needle

Freezer paper

Patterns:
◇ Fabric Quarter-Circle, page 107
◇ Freezer Paper Quarter-Circle, page 107
◇ Quilting Circle, page 107

## CUTTING INSTRUCTIONS

From the black with white prints, cut:
◇ Four 7½" squares *from each fabric*

From the black-and-white print, cut:
◇ One 16½" x 58½" backing

From the red, cut:
◇ Four 2¼" x 38" binding strips

*The unique circle pattern makes a striking runner for the dining table. The contrasting binding and buttons are the perfect finishing touches.*

1. Use the fabric quarter-circle pattern to cut four quarter-circles from each of the four white prints.

2. Use the freezer paper quarter-circle pattern to cut out several freezer paper templates. *Note:* The freezer paper can be re-used several times so it's not necessary to cut sixteen templates.

3. Iron a freezer paper template to the wrong side of a fabric quarter-circle, matching the corner and straight sides. Fold the extra ¼" of fabric over the curved edge of the paper and press. You may prefer to baste it before pressing.

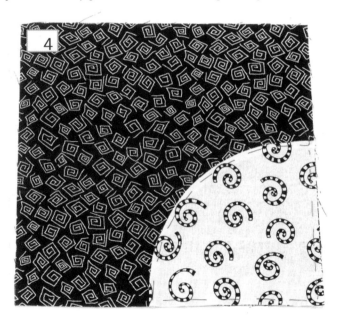

4. Remove the basting stitches and the paper and pin a quarter-circle to a black square in one corner. Baste the quarter-circle in place. Repeat to make a total of sixteen blocks, four blocks of each combination.

5. Appliqué the curved section of the quarter-circle to the background on each block. Do not remove the basting stitches at this time.

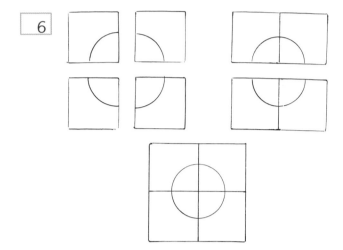

6. Arrange four different squares together with the appliqués forming a circle (A). Sew two squares, right sides together, for the top row and the remaining two squares together to form the bottom row (B). Press the seams open. Sew the two rows together to form a 14½" square with a circle in the middle (C). Press the seams open and remove the basting stitches on the circle. Repeat to make a total of four blocks.

7. Keeping the prints in the same order, sew the four blocks together end-to-end to make a runner 14½" wide and 56½" long.

8. Layer the backing, batting and pieced top following the Backing, Batting and Basting instructions on page 9.

9. Prepare the red binding and sew it to the runner following the Applied Binding instructions on page 10. Before folding the binding over to the back side, trim the batting and backing fabric even with the top.

10. Using black quilting thread, hand quilt around each appliquéd circle.

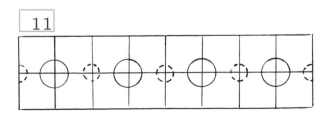

11. Use the quilting circle pattern to cut four freezer paper circles; cut one circle in half. Press a circle to the intersection of the blocks and a half circle at each end. Use these as patterns and quilt around each one.

12. Sew a red button to the center of each appliquéd circle.

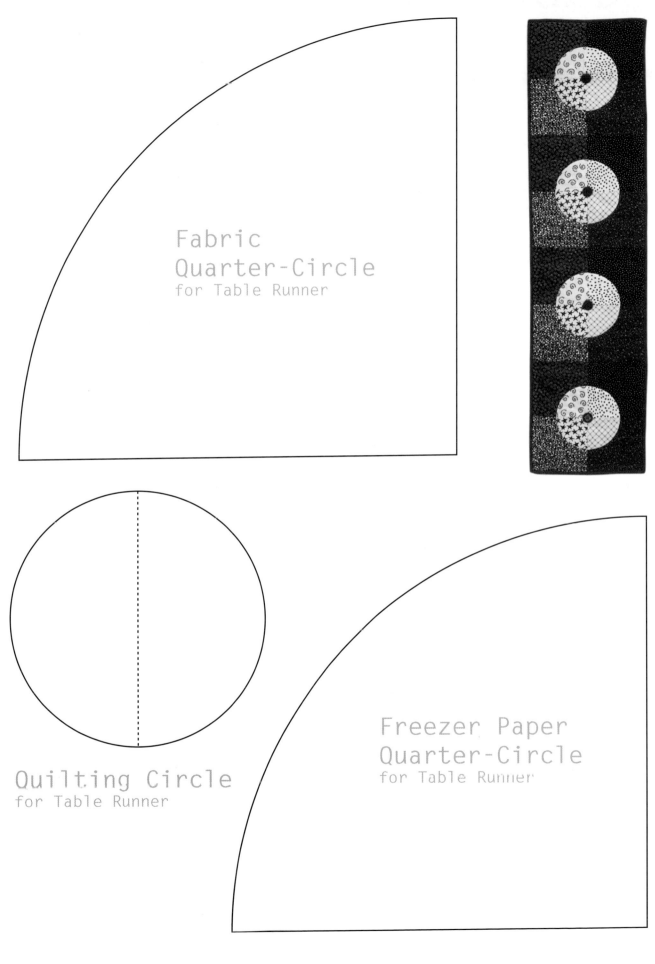

Fabric
Quarter-Circle
for Table Runner

Quilting Circle
for Table Runner

Freezer Paper
Quarter-Circle
for Table Runner

# Napkin, Place Card and Rose Corsage/Boutonnière

Finished size:
16" square napkin

## MATERIALS

(for one napkin, one place card and
one flower)

Fabric:
- ◇ Fat quarter black with white print
- ◇ Fat quarter white with black print
- ◇ Scrap of black felt

Matching sewing threads

Pre-made red chiffon ribbon rose,
2½" diameter

16" green wire-edged ribbon, 1⅞" wide

Pearl corsage pin

Cardstock:
- ◇ 4" x 3" black
- ◇ 3" x 2" red
- ◇ White

Black calligraphy pen or computer font

Pearl and silver button, ⅝"
(with the shank removed)

Permanent fabric adhesive

## CUTTING INSTRUCTIONS

From the black with white print, cut:
- ◇ One 17" square

From the white with black print, cut:
- ◇ One 17" square

From the black felt, cut:
- ◇ One 1¼" diameter circle

*A reversible napkin with two of the contrasting black-and-white prints has a neat fold to show off the lining and to hold the place card. The corsage/boutonnière is a quick project using a pre-made rose and it makes a wonderful addition to the setting.*

# FLOWER INSTRUCTIONS

1. To make two leaves, cut the green ribbon in half. Fold one ribbon in half so the halves are side by side. Pull the wire from the two inner edges to gather the ribbon up the middle. Wrap the exposed wires around the raw edges of the ribbon. Repeat to make a second leaf. See Ribbon Rose Napkin Holder on page 65 for step-by-step photos.

2. Arrange the rose and two leaves on the black felt circles and glue in place. Insert the corsage pin.

## PLACE CARD INSTRUCTIONS

1. Write the name on the white cardstock with the black pen. *Note:* Another option is to choose a computer font and print the name on the cardstock.

2. Trim the name card to 1½" x 2½".

3. Center and glue the red cardstock to the black.

4. Glue the name card on top of the red.

5. Glue the button to the upper left corner.

## NAPKIN INSTRUCTIONS

Make the napkin from the two fabric squares by following the instructions for a Reversible Napkin on page 15. Topstitch with matching or contrasting thread.

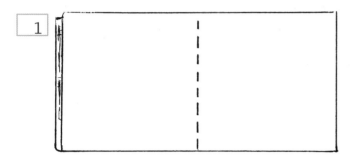

1. Fold the napkin in half and then in half again.

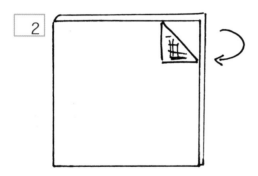

2. Turn down the top free corner about 1¾"; fold down two more times.

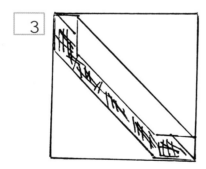

3. Turn the next free corner down in the same manner until it partially overlaps the first roll.

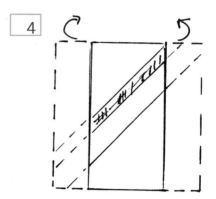

4. Fold under the top and the bottom of the napkin and turn it a quarter-turn to the left. The card can be placed in the fold with the flower resting on top.

# Wine Bag
Finished size: 16" high

## MATERIALS

Fabric:
- ◇ Two coordinating fat quarters of black and-white prints

3 pearl and silver buttons, ⅞" diameter

Red button, ½" diameter

½ yd. pearl trim on ribbon

1 yd. sheer red ribbon, 1½" wide

Matching sewing threads

## CUTTING INSTRUCTIONS

From each black-and-white print, cut:
- ◇ One 17" square

*Even the wine bottle is dressed for a party. The pearl trim and pretty ribbon give this wine bag a touch of class. It's perfect as a hostess gift or for your own celebration.*

1. Pin the two fabric squares together and sew ½" seam around three sides, leaving one side open (top). Press under the ½" seam allowance along the open end. Trim the corners and turn the bag right-side out.

2. Place the bag on your work surface, right-side up, with the opening at the top. The fabric showing on top will be the outside of the bag. Fold both sides inward so they overlap 2½" in the center; pin the fold to hold it in place.

3. Sew ½" seam at the bottom through all the layers.

4. To make a "box" bottom, flatten the bottom seam at one end to the side seam of the bag, matching the seam lines and forming a point. Sew across the bottom seam, 1" from the point. Repeat on the other side. Turn the bag right-side out.

5. To add the pearl trim, pin the ribbon between the two fabrics at the top with the pearls hanging out. Using a very small stitch, hand sew the two sides together with the ribbon remaining inside the seam.

6. To space the buttons and tie, place a wine bottle in the bag. Wrap the ribbon around the bag and the neck of the bottle, letting the top of the bag fold down. At the back of the bag, tack the ribbon in place. Cover the stitches with the red button.

7. Mark the position for the three pearl buttons down the center of the front. Remove the bottle and sew the buttons in place.

# Place Mat

Finished size: 15½" x 11½"

## MATERIALS

(for one place mat)

Fabric:
- ¼ yd. pink print for squares
- ½ yd. green print for top, backing and binding
- Scrap of yellow print

15½" x 11½" batting

Flat orange button, 1⅛" diameter

Matching sewing threads

Quilting threads for hand quilting:
- Pink
- Yellow

Quilting needle

Freezer paper

Patterns:
- Fabric Quarter-Circle, page 115
- Freezer Paper Quarter-Circle, page 115
- Quilting Circle 1, page 115
- Quilting Circle 2, page 115
- Quilting Circle 3, page 115

## CUTTING INSTRUCTIONS

From the pink print, cut:
- Four 6" squares

From the green print, cut:
- One 4½" x 11½" strip
- One 15½" x 11½" backing
- Two 2¼" x 32" binding strips

*This place mat's vibrant fabrics give it a very different look than the table runner. The circle pattern is still a dominant feature, but the mood is bright and easy going.*

1. Use the fabric quarter-circle pattern to cut four quarter-circles from the yellow fabric.

2. Use the freezer paper quarter-circle pattern to cut four quarter-circles from the freezer paper.

3. Iron a freezer paper template to the wrong side of a fabric quarter-circle, matching the corner and straight sides. Fold the extra ¼" of fabric over the curved edge of the paper and press. You may prefer to baste it before pressing.

4. Remove the basting stitches and the paper and pin a quarter-circle to a pink square in one corner. Baste the quarter-circle in place. Repeat to make a total of four blocks.

5. Appliqué the curved section of the quarter-circle to the background on each block. Do not remove the basting stitches at this time.

6. Arrange the four blocks together so the appliqués form a circle in the center. Pin two blocks together, right sides together and sew; press the seams open. Repeat for the remaining two blocks.

7. Sew the two rows together to make an 11½" square. Press the seam open and remove the basting stitches.

8. Sew the 4½" x 11½" green strip to one side of the circle block. Press the seam to the green side.

9. Assemble the layers following the Backing, Batting and Binding instructions on page 9.

10. Prepare and add the binding to the edges following the Applied Binding instructions on page 10.

11. Quilt around the appliquéd circles and between the green and the pink sections with pink quilting thread.

12. Use the quilting circle patterns to cut circles from freezer paper and iron them on the green section, with a large circle at the top and bottom and the other two in the middle. Quilt around these circles with yellow quilting thread. Remove the patterns.

13. Sew the orange button to the center of the yellow circle.

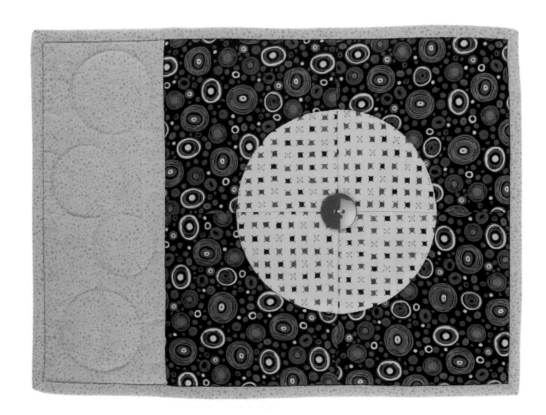

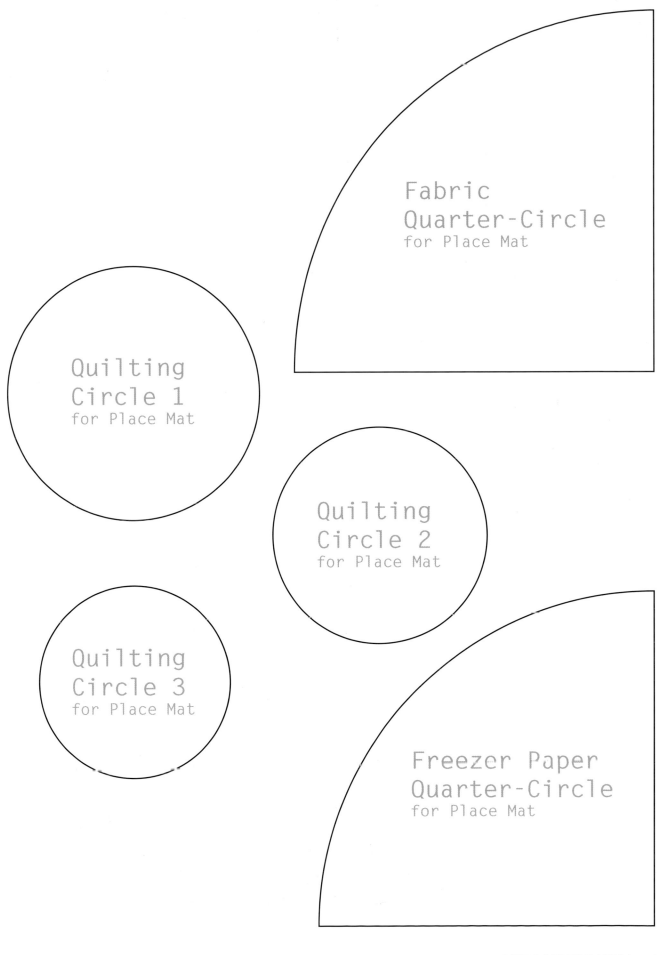

Fabric
Quarter-Circle
for Place Mat

Quilting
Circle 1
for Place Mat

Quilting
Circle 2
for Place Mat

Quilting
Circle 3
for Place Mat

Freezer Paper
Quarter-Circle
for Place Mat

# Reversible Napkin and Daisy Corsage/Boutonnière

Finished size:
16" square napkin

## MATERIALS

(for one napkin and one flower)

Fabric:
- ◇ Fat quarter green print
- ◇ Fat quarter yellow print

Wire-edged ribbon:
- ◇ 16" green
- ◇ 24" pink-and-yellow

Silk daisy

12" length of 20-gauge wire

White floral tape

Pearl corsage pin

Matching sewing threads

Permanent fabric adhesive

Pencil

## CUTTING INSTRUCTIONS

From the green print, cut:
- ◇ One 17" square

From the yellow print, cut:
- ◇ One 17" square

*Liven up your party with this whimsical daisy. The bright colors coordinate with the place mat.*

## FLOWER INSTRUCTIONS

1. Cut the green ribbon in half to make two 8" lengths. Fold one ribbon in half so the halves are side by side. Pull the wire from the two inner edges together to gather the ribbon up the middle. Wrap the exposed wires around the raw edges of the ribbon. Repeat to make a second leaf. See Ribbon Rose Napkin Holder on page 65 for step-by-step photos.

2. Cut the stem of the flower down to 1".

3. Use a thread and needle to add the leaves to the base of the flower.

4. Glue the top of the wire to the flower stem.

5. When the glue is set, wrap the stem and all of the wire with white floral tape.

6. Curl the wire by wrapping it around a pencil.

## NAPKIN INSTRUCTIONS

Refer to the instructions to make a Reversible Napkin on page 15 to make the napkin using the two fabric squares.

1. Fold the napkin in half one time.

2. Fold down one edge about 2" so the lining shows.

3. Fold the napkin in half so it forms a square.

4. Fold the two sides back.

5. Wrap the pink and yellow ribbon around it and tie the ends in a single knot.

6. Place the flower on top with a corsage pin.

# Card Party

Take the folding table and chairs out of the closet and dress them up for your next card party. This felt grouping is easy to make and really spruces up that boring table and chairs, making them look like part of the room décor.

## FABRIC SELECTION

Felt is a great choice for a card table cover because it drapes well and prevents the cards from sliding off to the floor. The color scheme and motifs can really coordinate with the game of choice. This table is set for a ladies' game of bridge with felt in cream, rose and leaf green with flower motifs. For a poker party, start with a standard kelly green base and add motifs of hearts, spades, diamonds and clubs along the side.

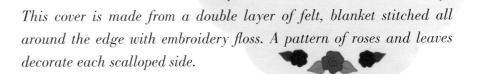

# Card Table Cover
Finished size: 54" square (to fit a standard 34" square table)

## MATERIALS

Felt:
- 3 yd. cream (54" wide)
- 9" x 12" sheets of felt:
  - Light rose
  - Dark rose
  - Light green
  - Dark green

Embroidery floss:
- Dark rose
- Light rose
- Dark green
- Light green
- Cream

10" x 34" piece of paper

Embroidery needle

Fade-out pen

White pencil

Freezer paper

Patterns:
- Large Flower, page 127
- Large Leaf, page 127
- Small Flower, page 126
- Small Leaf, page 127

## CUTTING INSTRUCTIONS

From the cream felt, cut:
- Two 54" squares

*This cover is made from a double layer of felt, blanket stitched all around the edge with embroidery floss. A pattern of roses and leaves decorate each scalloped side.*

1. Fold the paper in half so it measures 10" x 17".

2. Draw a gentle curve on a corner of the unfolded side of the paper.

3. Cut on the line and unfold the paper. This is the pattern for the scalloped sides of the cover.

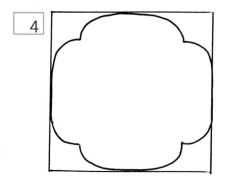

4. Layer the two cream felt squares and place the paper pattern centered along one side. Pin in place and cut along the curved edge. Unpin the pattern and move it to another side. Pin and cut again. Repeat until all four sides are cut.

5. Use the patterns to draw four large flowers, eight small flowers, eight small leaves and eight large leaves on the dull side of the freezer paper; cut out.

6. Iron the paper, shiny side down, to the felt, holding the iron about 3-4 seconds until the paper adheres, but still is easy to pull off. Cut out all the pieces, cutting through the paper and felt, and remove the paper patterns. *Note:* Use the following chart to iron the patterns to the colored felt:

| | |
|---|---|
| 4 large flowers | light rose |
| 8 small flowers | dark rose |
| 8 large leaves | light green |
| 8 small leaves | dark green |

7. Transfer the swirl pattern to the center of each flower using the fade-out pen on the light rose felt and the white pencil on the dark rose felt.

8. Stem stitch over the swirl lines using two strands of dark rose embroidery floss for the light flowers and two strands of light rose floss for the dark flowers.

9. Transfer the vein line down the center of each leaf with the fade-out pen on the light green felt and the white pencil on the dark green felt.

10. Stem stitch over the lines using two strands of dark green floss on the light leaves and two strands of light green floss on the dark leaves.

11. Arrange the appliqués on one of the felt covers. Center a large flower on one side, about 2⅝" up from the bottom edge. Refer to the photo and arrange the light leaves on either side of the flower, with the wide end of the leaves under the flower edge. Place a dark flower and a dark leaf on each side of the center flower. Pin the appliqués in place. Repeat for each side.

12. Using three strands of floss, blanket stitch each felt appliqué to the table cover, using the same color floss as you used for the stem stitch.

13. Pin the second felt table cover to the back of the appliquéd piece.

14. Using three strands of cream floss, blanket stitch all around the edges through both layers.

# Chair Back Covers
Finished size: 19" x 8½"

## MATERIALS

(for one cover)

Felt:
- ¼ yd. cream (54" wide)
- Scrap of light rose
- Scrap of light green

Embroidery floss:
- Dark rose
- Dark green
- Cream

20" x 9" piece of paper for the pattern

Cream-colored sewing thread

Embroidery needle

Fade-out pen

Freezer paper

Patterns:
- Large Flower, page 127
- Large Leaf, page 127

*A little appliqué, one seam and blanket stitched edges are all it takes to make a cover for the back of a folding chair.*

1. Fold the paper in half so it measures 10" x 9".

2. Use the back of the chair as a guide to draw a curve on the unfolded side of the paper. Cut along this line to make the pattern.

3. Use the paper pattern to cut two pieces from the cream felt.

4. Use the flower and leaf patterns to draw one large flower and two large leaves on the dull side of the freezer paper; cut out.

5. Iron the paper, shiny side down, to the felt, holding the iron about 3-4 seconds until the paper adheres, but is still easy to pull off. Cut out all the pieces, cutting through the paper and felt, and remove the paper patterns. *Note:* Use the following chart to iron the patterns to the colored felt:

| 1 large flower | light rose |
| 2 large leaves | light green |

6. Transfer the swirl pattern to the center of each flower using the fade-out pen.

7. Stem stitch over the swirl lines using two strands of dark rose embroidery floss.

8. Transfer the vein line down the center of each leaf with the fade-out pen.

9. Stem stitch over the lines using two strands of dark green floss.

10. Pin the rose to the center of the chair cover with a leaf on each side. Blanket stitch the appliqués in place with three strands of floss.

11. Pin the two cover pieces together, right sides together, and sew ½" seam around the sides and top, leaving the bottom open. Clip the curves and turn right-side out.

12. Using three strands of cream floss, blanket stitch the bottom edge all around to finish the cover.

## MATERIALS

(for two)

Felt:
- ◇ Scrap of light rose
- ◇ Scrap of dark rose
- ◇ Scrap of light green
- ◇ Scrap of dark green

Embroidery floss:
- ◇ Light rose
- ◇ Dark rose
- ◇ Light green
- ◇ Dark green

Embroidery needle

Fade-out pen

White pencil

Freezer paper

Patterns:
- ◇ Large Flower, page 127
- ◇ Large Leaf, page 127

*This is a little project that you can carry around to work on whenever you have a few minutes—and you will have a stack of coasters ready to use in no time. These are made to coordinate with the card table and chair covers, but could be made in any color combination for everyday use.*

1. Draw four large flowers and two large leaves on the dull side of the freezer paper.

2. Iron the paper, shiny side down, to the felt, holding the iron about 3-4 seconds until the paper adheres, but still is easy to pull off. Cut out all the pieces, cutting through the paper and felt, and remove the paper patterns. *Note:* Use the following chart to iron the patterns to the colored felt:

| 2 large flowers | light rose |
|---|---|
| 2 large flowers | dark rose |
| 1 large leaf | light green |
| 1 large leaf | dark green |

3. Transfer the swirl pattern to the center of each flower using the fade-out pen on the light rose felt and the white pencil on the dark rose felt.

4. Stem stitch over the swirl lines using two strands of dark rose embroidery floss for the light flowers and two strands of light rose floss for the dark flowers.

5. Transfer the vein line down the center of each leaf using the fade-out pen on the light green felt and the white pencil on the dark green felt.

6. Stem stitch over the lines using two strands of dark green floss on the light leaves and two strands of light green floss on the dark leaves.

7. Using three strands of floss, blanket stitch around a single leaf with dark green for the light leaf and light green for the dark leaf.

8. Pin the two matching flowers together with the embroidered side up. Slip the wide edge of the leaf between the two layers as you pin. Add a light green leaf to the light flower and a dark leaf to the dark flower.

9. Blanket stitch all around the edge of the flower, catching the leaf in the stitches.

# Tally Book
Finished size: 3¼" x 5¼"

## MATERIALS

Felt:
- ◇ 9" x 12" sheet of light rose
- ◇ Scrap of dark rose

Embroidery floss:
- ◇ Black
- ◇ Light rose
- ◇ Dark rose

3" x 5" pad of paper

Embroidery needle

Fade-out pen

White pencil

Freezer paper

Permanent fabric adhesive or double-stick tape

Patterns:
- ◇ Flower, page 126
- ◇ Tally, page 127

*This simple cover is made to fit over a pad of paper or score pad. It's quick and can be re-used over a fresh pad.*

1. Measure the spine of your pad of paper. Cut two pieces of light rose felt 3¼" wide x 10¼" plus the spine measurement long. (The pad in the model is 3" x 5" with a ⅜" spine. The felt was cut 3¼" x 10⅝".)

2. Draw one small flower on the dull side of the freezer paper. Iron it to the dark rose felt and cut it out.

3. Transfer the swirl lines to the flower with the white pencil and stem stitch over the lines with two strands of light rose floss.

4. Transfer the word "Tally" to one end of one of the felt rectangles with the fade-out pen. Backstitch over the lines with two strands of black floss. Make a French knot at the letter ends for dots.

5. Pin the flower appliqué above the word and blanket stitch all around the edges with three strands of light rose floss.

6. Pin the two rectangles together with the appliquéd side on top and blanket stitch the edges together using three strands of dark rose floss.

7. Use permanent fabric adhesive or double-stick tape to attach the back inside cover to the back of the pad. Flip the cover over to the front.

Small Flower
for Card Table Cover

Flower
for Tally Book

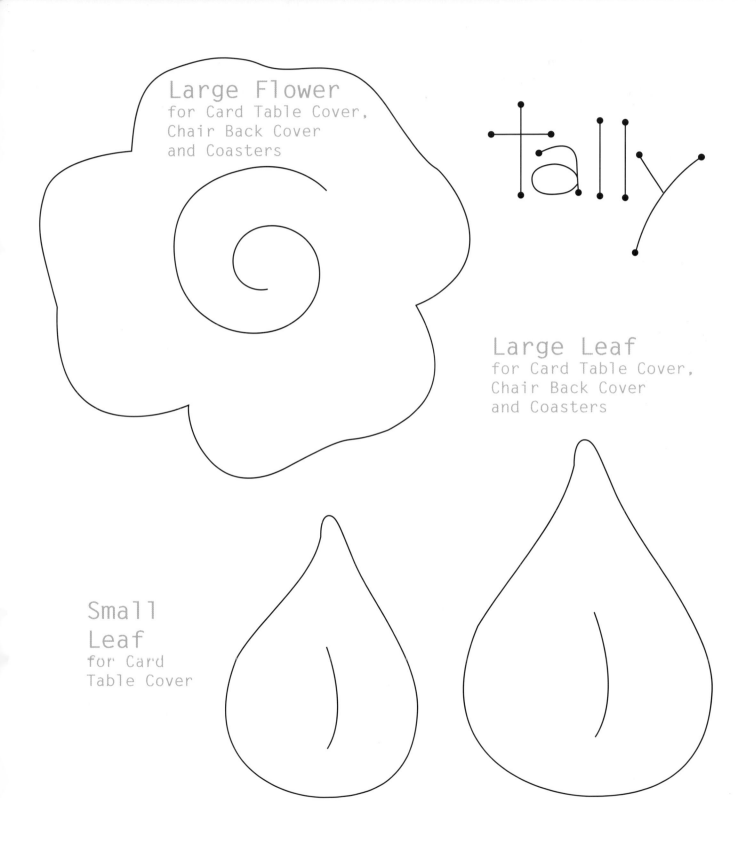

Large Flower
for Card Table Cover,
Chair Back Cover
and Coasters

tally

Large Leaf
for Card Table Cover,
Chair Back Cover
and Coasters

Small
Leaf
for Card
Table Cover

# Resources

Beacon Adhesives, Inc.
Beacon Chemical Co.
P.O. Box 10550
Mt. Vernon, NY 10550
(914) 699-3400
http://www.beaconcreates.com
Fabri-Tac™ Permanent Adhesive

DMC® Corp
S. Hackensack Avenue
Port Kearny Building #10-F
South Kearny, NJ 07032
(973) 589-0606
http://www.dmc-usa.com
Embroidery floss, pearl cotton, quilting
thread

Delta Technical Coatings, Inc.
2550 Pellissier Pl.
Whittier, CA 90601
(562) 695-7969
http://www.deltacrafts.com
Perm Enamel™ Paint for Glass

Fairfield Processing Corp
P.O. Box 1157
Danbury, CT 06813
(203) 744-2090
http://www.poly-fil.com
Poly-fil Extra Loft Batting

Fredericksburg Rugs™
P.O. Box 649
Fredericksburg, TX 78624
(800) 331-5213
http://www.fredericksburgrugs.com
Rug making supplies

Hansen's Brand Source
990 W. Fulton St.
Waupaca, WI 54981
(715) 258-7803
http://www.homeappliances.com/hansen

Krylon®
Sherwin-Williams Diversified Brands,
Inc.
101 Prospect Ave. NW
Cleveland, OH 44115
(216) 566-2000
http://www.krylon.com
Make It Suede™, Matte Finish

Plaid® Enterprises, Inc.
3225 Westech Dr.
Norcross, GA 30092
(678) 291-8100
http://www.plaidonline.com
Bucilla® Pure Silk Ribbon
Folk Art Acrylic Paints, Indoor/Outdoor
Gloss™ Acrylic Enamel, Royal Coat®
Decoupage Finish, Simply® Stamps
"Buggy" ant stamp

Prym-Dritz Corp.
P.O. Box 5028
Spartanburg, SC 29304
(864) 576-5050
http://www.dritz.com
Fray Check™

The Warm™ Company
954 E. Union St.
Seattle, WA 98122
(206) 320-9276
http://www.warmcompany.com
Soft & Bright™ Needled Polyester
Batting

Therm O Web
770 Glenn Ave.
Wheeling, IL 60090
(800) 323-0799
http://www.thermoweb.com
HeatnBond® Iron On Adhesive Lite,
Ultra Hold

Walnut Hollow®
1409 State Road 23
Dodgeville, WI 53533
(800) 395-5995
http://www.walnuthollow.com
Wood serving tray, wood memo holder
with pad

Wrights®
P.O. Box 398
West Warren, MA 01092
(800) 628-9362
http://www.wrights.com
Maxi piping, jumbo rickrack, bias tape

# About the Author

Starting with 4-H as a young girl, Chris has been sewing and crafting most of her life. She has been designing professionally for over ten years and has had hundreds of her projects published in magazines and books. She is the author of several soft-cover books on sewing and quilting. For fun, she enjoys tinkering with mixed media art and collecting antique sewing notions. Chris lives on the beautiful southern Oregon coast.